Intro To
GROUP THERAPY

SEQUOIA RAMIREZ

Intro To Group Therapy

©2021 Sequoia Ramirez

print ISBN: 978-1-09839-785-2

ebook ISBN: 978-1-09839-786-9

CONTENTS

WHAT KEPT ME GOING
(WHEN OTHERS TOLD ME TO STOP)

Professor Ojikutu (a black man at a predominantly white school, DePaul University, who saw my discussions during my Chicago bronzeville conversations and always had the kindest smile

> Ms. Ramirez,
>
> Speaking as 1) a writer, 2) an avid reader, and 3) your instructor, both of your essay submissions in this course are stunning in their quality. Here, now, beyond the end of the quarter, I understand that you are working a rather taxing job while attending the university. I understand this as a trial undertaken by many students attending an institution such as DePaul.
>
> That said, as per my own observations of your in-class contributions and the substance of your submitted work, you are an A-level student at university level.
>
> So, I beseech you, Ms. Ramirez, do not stop, do not be dissuaded, do not undersell yourself here at this institution, nor at any further stop along your path. You have so very much to offer the domain of knowledge, information, practice, critical thought, craft and creation. You can do great things. If you please do those things along your way, your better interests will be served. Continued light. .
>
> Always,
>
> Professor Ojikutu

Professor Choi (an Asian scriptwriting class professor, who even entered my work into a selection service for senior graduates and mine got in)

> This is really good Sequoia. Really sweet. You have a great voice and your voice is authentic. I really hope you continue to write and I look forward to how you develop in the coming years as a filmmaker. Keep up the great work and thanks for a great quarter!

Professor Kummin (who taught History of Cinema, who reached out to me out of concern when I didn't turn in my final for weeks after having a major mental health crisis with Imposter Syndrome)

> This is excellent work. Your analysis of each film is deep and insightful, you apply each of your arguments well, and you pull lots of support through examples in the film and your research. Very well done!

> Sequoia - Overall, this is pretty solid. You definitely do a great job of exploring how the personal lives of the directors impacted their work. Your exploration of the socio-political aspects of the films is well done. I think over all, the paper could have used another thorough edit: there are a few spelling errors and the wording is sometimes clunky. Other than that, though, well done. - Ben

> - 2 for late submission

Professor Matei (a quirky man who let me and Leah turn in our animation late because he loved us and understood our strife)

Dr. Williams (who after taking her environmental Biology class and aided in a presentation of climate change but correlated it with Veganism and Anti-blackness, offered to write a letter of recommendation for wherever I go.)

*Mr. Urban (*a white man who was the first adult in my education at a predominantly black and brown high school, who prioritized the literature in casting me in *The House On Mango Street* and *Into the Beautiful North,* along with countless *poc* narratives that helped me find and love myself in the fullest extent.

Dzurison (who pushed me beyond the imaginary limits I had for myself. Thank you for everything, old man.

*Mrs. Kledzick (*a white woman who casted me in plays and always saw in me what was hard for me to see in myself.)

Mrs. Durning (a woman who constantly pushed me to use my voice in any way I could, even when my grades were slipping.)

*Mrs. Filo (*a short and witty woman who was the first person to call my writing trash so that it could be better. I worked so hard just to have her smile at a paper.)

*Dinah Clottey (*a young black woman who had the same voice and interest as me, but British, who held me up when even those I loved held me down. She never had to be told to love me out loud. She was the Valedictorian of our class.)`

Cherith Clottey: (a young black woman who was the best artist I had ever seen and held me up. A woman who aided me in illustrating the work you read. She was in the top of our class.)

Halle Clottey (a young black woman who embodied power in all ways and continued to push boundaries in all areas. She was the Valedictorian of her class.)

Carmen Ortiz (who was my home away from home when I didn't have one, and opened up her doors to me when I had nowhere to sleep at night when I was living out of the district and sometimes faced homelessness.)

Cristian Mora (someone who was my partner in life and related to me when I didn't feel heard the most. He was also my partner in acting and is following an acting and movie making career on his own.)

Jillian Harris (a childhood church class friend, who no matter what life threw at us, always ended up back in my life and with love.)

Dakota Johnson (a young man who remained as a home and neutralizer for me when no one else answered my calls to cry.)

Alexcia Lira (who repeated to me my worth, when others repeated to me my lack thereof.

Arei Richardson (who filled me with hope that I could change the world.)

Leah Tibebu (a young Ethiopian woman who also felt my strife of going to a private institution and even when we left and went our separate ways, and continued to love me miles apart.)

Kendall Alexander Oliver (who loved me with all that was possible of him, even when he feared love itself.)

Janeen Shante Ashley (My Mom) (who advocated for me and broke down the same walls she faced all her life. To the woman who took her broken dreams and implanted them in me in the form of seeds. I love you.)

Miguel Ramirez (My Dad) (who came to every play, game, marching competition, and speech or GI competition. You cheered me on even when I played the bassoon and I love you.)

My Abuelita Vicenta (who gave me love and a home in eyes. That language alone could never stop. My inspiration for all the things that I do. I love you.)

The Memory of My Grandma Norma Ashley (Winkie): (for teaching me the importance of love in a world raised to hate. For coming to me even after death and giving me all the hugs and strength I needed to carry on.)

For my Papa Vincent Ashley (for always sharing your wide smile whenever you were proud of me, or for always treating me since I was a little kid, that I was destined for true greatness.)

My Auntie Jazzmin: (who taught me the art of resilience, even when your own family wishes to see you fail. You taught me to never give up, and to always spread joy when the world around you begins to crumble.)

My Kids at Eisenhower (who let me learn how to be a mother before becoming one on my own.)

My Acting Teacher at John Casa Blancas (who knew of my financial situation and saw the way kids would not eat with me. As a black woman herself filled me with encouragement and wisdom as we'd split a sandwich during break. Even at six years old and only being able to afford to be there for less than a year, her words carry me today.)

My Little Sister Mariah (who taught me more about self-worth than I could have taught myself.)

My Older Brother Tony (who showed me what inner peace and knowing your limits meant, and the importance of continual education.)

My Cousin Bray (for never hesitating to pull me aside and talk when he knew I felt out of place.)

To My Aunty Cashawn (for making fun vegan dishes with me and laughing even as you told me your inner pains.)

My cousins Cameron And Courtney (who let me hold onto their hands and sit on their lap as we rode to the cemetery to bury Grandma. You both made me feel safe.)

To Sunni (for being our spiritual warrior when our house needed you most.)

Mrs. Maravillas (who let me use her office as a therapy session when all I wanted to do was cry where the world couldn't see me.)

Dr. Antos (who trusted a young girl he barely knew to teach herself how to play the bassoon in two months.)

Denise and Tony (who at a church event to give back and held my hand while others yelled.)

And to you (for reading my book, when I thought the idea was too far from my grasp.)

And many, many more when I just felt like giving up

Part One:

SELF

(A self-analysis of who we are)

*A look into not only the divide between me and you,
but further want of education of how I even degrade myself
in my own pew.*

Freshman

If we could simply live multiple lives, then I would have lived them all,
The one with the college life and dorms that ring
Tangled up thoughts and emotions on screen.
I think I'd have been loved and the one to give love
In these condensed cases of things that no longer hold magic or mystery,
When the curtains are pulled and everything seems mundane or normal,
I think back to the lives and how all I wished I had lived.

Something's Off

How do I begin to feel real again?
At night when the sun's gone away and everyone else's days begin to fade
Into their phones and their successes all dolled up in dresses.
Telling myself that life isn't a race,
But not to take my time on this earth for granted.
I don't want to be known for my forgetting,
For people looking at me and wondering where did things
Go wrong.
When did I give up on fulfilling everyone else's dreams for me?
Sitting on the sidelines of everyone else's breakout moments that
Were once predicted to be shared amongst one another.
But my family needs me.
Or maybe I'm finally at a point in my life where I need them.
I don't think this feeling of dissatisfaction just goes away
You don't wake up and say
I'm happy with the mundane,
With the rising and making the rays shine for someone else's days.
While mine become bleaker as someone who's taken on the role of
a cheerleader,
On the bleachers scribbling my name into the hard exterior.
But also what a life it would be if I were
Finally set free from everyone else's eyes,
Or their long exasperated sighs, when I was supposed to "make it."
But grew tired from carrying the weight
And pushing against my fears with bottled up tears.
I don't think this feeling just vanishes,
Because if it did,
I would love to go along with it.

Empty Casket

I'll keep this between me and you.
I'll stop trying to fix my words and tie each letter
Together.
So that people can think I'm witty,
Or special,
Or wise.
Truthfully so,
Between the two of us,
There's this emptiness that I feel a lot of the time.
This feeling like there was this
Big,
Magnificent life that
I was supposed to live,
But I somehow missed it.
I was supposed to turn left, but I
Turned right.
The scrolls of my destiny said I'd pick blue
Instead of picking you.
That I'd press submit
Instead of saying maybe later.
And now I'm on this wonky path
That the universe had not intended for me.
That's why things feel so out of place,
Why the exhaustion in everyone's eyes feel so familiar.
Because I've taken on this melancholic limbo
That so many have fallen into.

In my dreams, I'll see everything
Like the vignettes
Passing by on this fading clip that gets smaller
And smaller as it fades in the distance.
Because the timeline of my dreams and who I am
In actuality
Are coming to be one,
And those pictures don't match
Like the one where I was college bound
For an ivy league with
Full ride scholarships.
Or the one where I'm in New York
Living on my own in a one bedroom flat,
And I have a cat
Called Susie that's black,
And I have this internship that's turning into a job.
I go to pretentious dinners and sip champagne,
And when I go home every blue moon
I realize that nothing has changed
But me —
And for the better.
If we're stopping the audience to only us
And you promise to never tell.
I love who I am,
But I'm not sure that's the person I'm supposed
To be.
Which is me.

I'll do something or I'll miss another deadline,
And I'll think,
There it is.
That's it.
That was the last straw.
The last attempt to save the wide eyes of hope.
I'm going to be stuck,
And I'll feel the fading fantasy.
The opening picture
Dissipating till barely visible, because I'm moving past the time of
Bringing it into light.
No more time or even want to speak things into fruition,
To pretend that the air is so still but that I'm
constantly moving.
I can feel myself
Sinking into the backdrop,
Until I'll become the fluff for the empty space
In someone else's big picture.
So,
If I reach my hand out to you and you
Reach your hand out to me,
Then maybe it's a possibility
That our fears aren't too far apart.

Moon Cheese

Do you ever wonder what's up there?
Sit and stare into the night sky,
And wonder if somewhere light years away
There's another person staring right at you,
Looking lovingly into the moonlight.
Just like you.
Praying for an answer.
Am I going anywhere in this life,
Or does any of it really matter?
And what if that answer was only covered by a thin veil,
And all you had to do
Was reach out and touch?

Shortcomings

Can I speak my truth?
About how this feeling of disappointment in myself
Is in a constant loop
Of short comings and tiny successes,
But none big enough to keep me from stressing.
About how I'm supposed to pull my family out of the
Mud,
When I use it as a mask when I sleep.
This self-sabotage is rooted too deep for me to see
That I am good enough
To stop putting bricks in my path to trip on,
So that people stop expecting me to reach the finish line.
I can't fail if I make sure I block my time,
Block my blessings,
And start by addressing the fact that
I know I can make it.
My veins may be filled with magic,
But I'm as real as the tears on your cheek
When you get scared of all that potential
That might not manifest into something active.
Rather than untapped gold that first started off
As a braggard's tune
But was molded into a burden by its creators hands,
I truly apologize to the younger me
Who so badly wanted to be
A future me,
Who thought she had success that would stretch beyond the sea,

But maybe that vision needs to be postponed.
Maybe that idea I should allow to be
Taken out on a loan
To my nieces and my nephews,
Who need something to get them through the night.
I can feel my blessings at the parting of my lips
Like each tear,
Each break between breaths.
For the flood to flow and wipe away
All that I had become accustomed to
For my dreams to take flight without faulty wings.
But I need to understand that God can only
Get me so far.
He can only show me the way, but he can't push my feet, or
Break the bonds that I have for years forged.
You want so badly to be all that you know you can.
You sit up at night and see the ones you love.
That reach to the lower back.
They squeeze
Because they're scared this time
They might break.
But, look.
Turn those eyes inward.
The cracks in your bones rattle, too,
And the weight of all that you wish to accumulate
Without time
Will cause the final break,
And all that will be left will be the shell of the human you once were.

My Own Keeper

To the younger me
Who thought that life
Would come to her so easily—
I'm sorry.
I'm sorry I gained reality
And allowed self-doubt
To destabilize my mentality,
To go from being destined for greatness
To accepting chance,
And the way it is
Not for me if it's given.
To another girl who's house remained hidden
From misfortune and grief,
That took its toll on not just me,
But on the women I looked to be family
And crumpled rocks like sheet paper.
When shared wealth was not solely theirs to see.
I think I mean
To seek forgiveness for the things
I allowed to trample our tracks.

Making mistakes without looking back
And wondering if that small girl still thought
She could take on the world.
Replay the tapes
And read back the captions.
Keep studying their faces,
And wishing you could take action
In front of an audience that's all packed in
Like sardines in a tin can.
To see you on stage just acting
To that little round face
And a million dreams to chase.
Of being an inventor, a singer, an actor.
I send my greatest sorrows
To a younger me who never counted.
Growing up
As a factor.

Stay

If emotions could be painted across the skies
Like a mosaic of the things in my mind—
Would you hear the heartbreak a thousand times?
Would you see the tears too dry in my eyes
To fall or bring out the things I feel inside
So that they'll stop collecting inside
Like pebbles and stones all waiting to
Topple over?
If I stayed where I am and became very quiet
And thanked for my blessings, would that mean
All was a blessing
To form growth?
I sound depressing.
I must sound like a broken spirit
Like a new kite cut down and taped and thrown into the air too soon.
I'm stuck
Between who I was and who I need to be,
For more than just my family,
But the girl inside who felt like she could never be
The one who was first pick,
And not some annoying thing
Some stupid thing.
Some worthless over capacity
Burden thing.

If I stay right here and I close my eyes,
And I hope that things could just be easy—
To be like the girls I know who walk through life so freely.
Or maybe if I cried then I'd feel more alive,
Look down on myself
And wonder if I should just die.
While I still have some greatness to dwindle
And so people can say she died before her time and not that she missed
her prime like
The 9 AM train on the redline.
Maybe if I stayed and let life carry me,
Not take anything personally,
Just see how it all ends and wonder if it was destiny.
For me to always be uneased,
To always end up at this point
Of flight or fight.
Get it wrong.
Get it right.
Drop out.
Don't drop out. You need to be in school.
If you're not, they'll call you a fool.
But maybe you could use that as a tool.

Release

Why do people compare sadness to emptiness?
A void without an end.
But when I feel sad it feels
Heavy.
I feel overwhelmed by the flood gate that
Guards my heart.
Life doesn't feel real.
Every edge becomes sharper,
Crisper,
And my tears can't seem to escape fast enough
For the pressure to ease
For even a small moment of
Release.

Funny Bone

Why does sadness feel like funny dream,
Like the way you perceive is not the way it seems?
Like my heads wrong, it ain't screwed on?
I got bad thoughts, nobody knows what I mean.
I feel like I must being going mental.
The way my day ends,
It cause a tremble,
And I'm up all night just wondering
What contract somebody else got with the devil.
Did I wrong you in my past life?
Was it you at the hit and run last night?
Or am I just destined to experience growth
Like a fight for my rights with no medal?
It's hitting me in my dreams
The way I travel must mean something.
Or maybe I'm crazy. It's affecting me daily.
Things ain't always how they seem.
I'm in a dream.

A Disease

Have you ever missed someone
So bad
That you wished you'd never met them?
You wish you could go back to
The exact moment
They came into your life
And stop the collision—
The collision of two people
That would soon evolve to a
Supernatural connection.
A divine intervention
That can't possibly be
Real,
As if your feelings towards anyone else have been
Superficial,
And this was the first time you felt anything
Real.
And it's scary because
You can feel your heart so filled with
Adoration, love, and joy,
But on the edge of a shatter.

And in its fragility it can only be cradled
Or hardened
By simple actions of your correspondence.
Ever missed someone so much
You begin to question your health?
Like, hey, does it make sense that I miss
More than your lips
And more than a passionate kiss?
But the way you felt like the eight year old me
Got her every wish,
Or when you miss friends that you know aren't
Coming back.
And this feeling is so raw and so all consuming
That you don't know if it'd be better to
Not feel at all.
Or knowing you went the rest of your life
Knowing you had the chance to feel.
To actually feel something
And you ran away scared.

Hey Sweety

Hey sweety.
Are you still there?
I've been trying to show you that I care.
You won't let time tick you for the days.
Check here, check there.
You passed the safety test.
Your heart has been healed and I'll
Take care of the rest.
The other house doesn't hold a home
For the things you need to learn on your own.
Love within.
Stop seeking it in him.
The healing isn't plastered on his
youthful little face.
His kisses and his soft touch.
The pain he can't erase.
Stack them like pebbles and one day
They'll fall.
Crashing down.
Crashing down.
Can you handle it all?

Cranium

When I was younger,
There was a key lesson that I learned very early on.
There was something wrong with me.
I would go to class and when lunch came around,
I always ended up eating by myself
Or with the teacher.
I would run around playgrounds alone,
Afraid to skid my knees on the concrete,
But pushed by a peer to get to someone else.
Friends that told me I was just too much,
Or friends that would sit around another eight year old
And tell her to make her own friendship bracelet.
The only thing that changed when I got older
Was the cafeteria food.
The seats either left cold
Or filled with frigid bodies that falsely warmed me up.
You know when you spend so many years of your life
Being made to feel small,
It's hard to believe that someone
So small
Could be capable of such big things.
I never thought I could be capable of anything.
I wish I could see in me
The things people see shining from my being.
Am I talented,
Or am I spending so much time chasing the
Potential?
People claim I have.
Is it too late to make the mouse an elephant?

Tea Party

Ah yes, now gentleman how shall we—
Oh, and I do mean women as well.
As you shall be the first to deshell
The carcass of black women and steal the gold plated
Diamonds inside.
Reshape and rename them in your mind
In a way that we can sell.
Shall I start my formal address
To every person I call my guest?
Or have I caught you all in a moment of distress?
Or have you spotted one of the lot we do detest?
I will persist.
Tonight I call to you the moment in which
If I do
Call to order the consent over a greatest deal
In exchange for a free meal.
Pass the gravy and I'll give you fresh veal.
Oh, it is a chuckle, this whole ordeal.
I say to you petty guests
And all my loving ladies tied up in a dress,
We will never give their backs a rest,
As they carry out our every request.
Though I must digress.
We shall not provide idle time
For these people to form dreams and thoughts in their minds.
Let it be riddled with their lack of time
To even experience life without even the fraction of the money shared
between you and I.
Let our bellies come full with the sweetest cut
And their broad shoulders will fall like the mutts
To scrap the pennies we let fall from our pockets in order to calm their
screaming lower gut.

My fellow people, let them steer the wheel,
Then take pride in your stride as you see the repeating reel
Of bills not meet and land leveling.
Offer them the key
To afford their forgotten needs,
And watch your business flourish
From the blueprint they left behind.
Stop worrying about originality.
Their ancestors have gifted them the mentality
That hard work will soon pay off.
And by the time they realize—
Their time will have been bought with
Equality,
But never equity.
May I offer a toast,
A promise I hope we'll keep
Let them squander for their dreams
And let us wait for the perfect opportunity
To capture that shining gold,
Repurchased and then resold.
Rebranded and then rolled
in crisp brown paper bags.
It's the greatest idea I've had.
Yes, me.
It's the greatest trick you'll see.
A gift for one that will be
Passed down again and again all for free.
I hope you all enjoy the brie
Thank you for attending.
My annual tea party.

Eb

She stood drunken on false devotion.
Skin crawling with onlooker eyes.
Craving the very sheets that brushed her shoulder.
She found fascination in their gaze—
Found home in the scopes of their maze,
But never found justification for the misdeeds committed between
her waist.

Solemn Glory

I don't want to waste my time
Halfway gone with another candle blown.
Ever stand in the room that was molded in your vision?
Glasses clashing in heat over the fire you set
In people—
People who don't really know the fullness of
Your name,
Or all the mouths it stung with its venom.
All that work to create your perfect harmony of dreams.
Shouldn't you be happy?
Didn't all that work pay off?
Weren't all the sacrifices worth it?
Didn't you get every last thing you wanted for yourself?
What more could you crave?
You finally proved them wrong kid
So why doesn't it
Feel right?

I'm So Tired

Take a breath.
Slithering down and now it's lucid.
Sunken eyes.
Lids setting like the sun across the hill in my backyard.
Streets down and a zip code away from exoneration.
Frustration.
Feels like I'm sinking in a pool of my own
Darkest places and the tendencies tied to my soul.
My energy
Feels like someone stole my energy.
Sunny drives and hands out the window.
Now silent and slow and hunched in my seat.
Tucking my shirt in and in, pulling more because
I want to fold.
I want to turn inward,
My body curving in on itself and holding itself hostage, and yet
As a protector
I'm so tired.
Diagnosis?
Sleep deprivation.
But I don't need sleep. I need rest.
Rapid treatment of twenty-four hours could not be enough to cure or
subside my symptoms.
Hopeless, but not without a wish to be hopeful.
Tired, but with no want to gain that energy.
I'm so tired.
But pillows and soft cushions aren't the answer.

Nasty Nineteen

The weight of the world feels like paper thin whispers on your shoulder
when you've been carrying it for so long.
For a decade.
Purity and adolescence burnt from my eyes
At the knees of a father who didn't know
How to let go.
So he pleaded with his hands and made a
Simple demand
Of his ten-year-old daughter,
And a four year old strawberry shortcake with
Pink frost in her hair.
If only to see that the idea of a
Strong woman,
A numb woman,
No longer a pupil in a classroom without a guide.
Or a teacher.
I apologize for my misdemeanors.
If I acted young when I was meant to be an
Adult.
Mentally and emotionally for the young girl
Who I knew would still look to me to be her protector.
Feeling like loneliness wasn't a simple state that affected its host like a
passing plague
But rather a malignant tumor that grew
Over the years until it became
The reflection of who I was but never intended
To be.

Because being me had become a casualty
For those who saw me as too grown.
Trying to act too adult,
But never realized I wished to be
Fourteen when I was fourteen.
Fifteen when I was fifteen.
And to not be nineteen and feel like half my life is gone instead of a step
ahead and not a step into an
Endless abyss to more nothingness.
So loud until one day
Everyone had left because listening had become too
Troublesome.
So why talk?
Why open the gates and release all my secrets like
Wives tales and legends to those who needed
A light to illuminate their hidden path?
Everything moves in front of my eyes,
Faster than a hub of birds migrating for the new season—
Losing everything and wanting nothing more out of the ashes but the
gratuity I had gained.
I'm nineteen.
Sitting inside an extra storage unit
Watching the time topple over like dominos.
Nothing to my name
But frizzy hair and three tickets on my car.

Scary Cave

Just let me take things over from here.
I promise there's nothing for you to fear.
I'll take good care of our heart
And promise to never forget those days in art
Class when I couldn't mold clay into a single thing.
Remember when we'd run around
With our socks coming off
Into the pool with our blow up canoe.
We'd paddle all night,
Pretending to discover new lands,
But everything was always the same.
It just felt different.
You'll still be here.
I'll still hear you playing inside
With your plush black dog.
And I'll smile.
But it's time for you to go.
I loved you
And things ended too soon.
But it's time to move on.
Aren't you tired?
Come out of the dark
And into the light.
It's time to say goodnight.

12 Midnight

It's a new year so
It must be a new me.
A new decade
And a time to finally fulfill my dreams.
No more playground blues and shooting
For the hoop,
Thinking one day I'll do all the things
I want for myself now.
In the distance so far it's out of sight
Because I'm comfortable with putting the
Crushing weight of success
On the shoulders of a
Future me,
Who's potential has been postponed
Indefinitely.
I'll check on it tomorrow,
Crumple and wrinkle the timeline for today.
Let the flick of my wrist
Take a sour twist
Like the spoiled tofu in my Chinese takeout.
Throw it out.
Throw it up.
Check on it tomorrow because the future me is
Wiser.
Wiser than the miser that just wants to drown in the
Warmth
In the bottomless glass
Of red sangria in a room full of countdowns,
Cluttered like sardines all promising to be
The catch of day.
In the new day with new numbers at the tag line,
But the quality of the content the same.
It's a new year but I still feel
Like my clock didn't reach midnight.

Stay Home

When do the plateaus of our imagination
Meet invigoration?
When do the overly endowed cinema walls of my
Illuminated bedroom
Meet an audience of more than just one?
Is my mirror becoming crisper
Or am I facing an altered reality in which
My greatest companion
Is my never changing self-image?
When does the world end,
Or has it already ended?
And has my mind finally been destabilized
By the calendar in which I can no longer remember to
Mark down?
Is it art that I fester
An ongoing renaissance that I'll one day plaster around the world
For soulless eyes to see if only
To catch a glimpse of what temporary fated mortality looks like?
Am I creating what others have done in this type of self-induced
Isolation.
In this type of
Prison.
In this type of
Peace.

Maybe I've climbed to my peak.
Perhaps I have discovered an inner peace.
My ancestors have chosen to communicate with me
In ways that can only be reached in self-induced madness.
Can you hear the birds at night still singing their sunrise tunes?
I know you can hear them too.
Or the songs they sing only at noon,
But have somehow found the pitch
When the night's light that usually shines bright from the once
heavenly skies.
Stars by twilight
Have been
Extinguished.
Am I mad?
Or am I still grappling with the idea that what I've perceived as
normality or
Reality
Has all been based on a lie,
Or are there worse things beyond that door?
I think I'll stay inside.

Sometimes I Don't Like Me

I'm done trying to be poetic or be perfect or be wise.
I'm fucking sick of everyone thinking I have to talk or be entertaining all the time.
Or just be another convenient end to their day that they can shape and mold into every which way.
If I'm being honest I really want to go home, but I don't really know what home is.
I guess Home is me.
But what happens when the panels of my mind begin to rot away and all that is left is the girl I've never wanted to become.
That girl is so weak, so quiet, so hurt, so stupid,
But she's me.
She's who I've never wanted to be.
Everyone loves to hate me,
And they love to negate the fact that shit's fucked up for me too, but no one actually wants to listen.
They just want me to smile and be funny because I'm Sequoia and I'm too much in my feelings.
Sequoia, what the fuck kind of name is that?

A tree that's so strong inhabited by a dimwitted scared bitch named
Brianna who fits in with everyone but is important to no one.
I'm not important.
I'm just an extra in everyone's lives when they need someone to laugh at,
laugh with, but love to laugh without.
People use me for their fun, then throw me away when they're done with
My bag of tricks and the games and the things I provide
Are all gone and all that's left are the things on the inside.
When all that is left is me,
And no one wants to see a clown behind the scenes.
When the smile fades and the balloon animals won't twist,
So that I can't shape myself into what you consider a perfect fit.
They tell me they care, but I know they really fucking don't.
Because if they cared then they'd show it, they wouldn't treat me like my
words aren't valid, they wouldn't make me feel less than.
But maybe that's not a feeling,
Maybe it's a fact.

Big Heart

I really wish I had a big heart—
The authentic one that comes in a golden rimmed box.
Something pretty that wouldn't scare people away.
Safe and contained happiness for the world to share.
A memory recalled lovingly in the minds of those who only
Planted one foot in my path.
A nice girl
With a big heart that makes you smile.
But I've not given myself kindness so what makes you
The exception.

True Latino

You're a coconut!
Brown on the outside, white on the inside.
You're just playing, pretending to be someone you're not.
But I'm not!
I say my heritage is all that I got.
You stay silent, making prejudgments.
I say forget what you gotta say, can't I just be me.
Celebrating my culture and constantly trying to learn.
But you don't know Spanish! How you trying to learn when you can't
even understand.
I say language isn't the only thing that makes you drip from the land.
But it is! It's the way of our tongue,
Our ancestors passed it down for years
And you're the anomaly.
Anomaly?
Yeah, the one who sticks out.
A Latino without the language is like a hooker without a mouth.
Pointless, ironic, and better off dead. You'll never be a part of the struggle
when the real roots are what you've shed.
Roots? What makes you take part?
Oh, because you speak the true language than the culture is in your heart?
I call Bull!
I'm tired of you pretentious Latinos who act like you're ideal.
You fail to realize I know the real deal.
If we talking true Latino, then let's list all the requirements.
Racist, self-deprecating, and emotionally detached.

Wait, what?

Yeah I'm talking about the things we started doing way back.

Talking about, "Como Sali?" when a baby is born.

If the baby was born brown with nappy hair, then the family is torn

Between truly loving or hating the heritage, failing to realize what we all come from.

Black!

Naaaah.

Yes, you pretentious Latino with the ignorant mouth,

the natives, Africans, and Spaniards came together and we came

out! Latinos!

But the whiter the better!

And that's why you got only light skinned Latinos being showed in the media as-

True Latino!

What a manifestation of lies!

I'm claiming who we truly are, I'm done trying to deny.

Man, I'm the new aged Latino.

Make you realize your roots Latino,

Setting the standard for being a strong woman Latino.

Where we stop emotionally abusing our kids Latino,

Stop being secretly racist towards black people Latino,

Owning up to all of the prejudices Latino,

Trying to make a better generation for this world Latino,

Claiming who we really are Latino,

Where learning the language shouldn't be the only thing that makes you Latino.

Afro Latina

In Chicago streets you claim my fellow men.
I swallow the past offenses.
Within the racist regulations,
You don't want to build bridges,
But fences.
Lead me on my way I say,
Clasping onto yesterday.
The media cloud flashes blue and red sirens,
It must be time to pray.
I take out all of my religious candles
And hope you won't storm in.
You're illegal.
You're a rapist.
You're a wanted bandit.
My familia came here for opportunity,
Not for your scapegoating practices.
I sit here with olive skin,
And knit curls,
Awaiting the final storm.
I feel my identity is torn.
I'm not allowed to be proud.
I'm viewed as an alien on the soil where I was born.

Black Woman/Black Magic

(Written the Sunday Morning After Chicago Protest 4 A.M.)

I cannot spell it out for you.
My words would call it betrayal
When my lips form to spew out my experiences, my heartache, and my
silent sorrows.
Your ears only dazzle upon the gold you see in the potential of my brand.
You hold my hand as we walk but once my side of the road begins to
divert and crack.
You let go
And I am left to fall
Into an endless abyss that I never knew you spent years digging for me.
For table talks with my grandmother
And cups of chamomile with my mother. When the tv screams at me my
own face or my brothers or my sisters
Dead in the same playgrounds they once frolicked.
Letting years compile, and realizing one day the weight of comment your
children whispered to me in the middle of show and tell.
When my throat tightens and my lips become chapped,
I call to you for only a sip of the water you make seem glorious.
The drink from your cup runneth over
And my cup which runs empty.
You teach me to hate my cup.
Hate it's pattern.
But teach me that it's my reality.
It is normal,
But it is completely my fault.
When I reach out for you when my roads diverge and mine is riddled
with danger
You let go,
Distracted by the light of your unbarred future.
December 21, 1999, in a hospital in Berwyn Illinois, Brianna Elena
Ramirez was born. Named after her uncle who left this earth too soon,
Brian. And her great grandmother the activist and caregiver- Elena.
My family surrounded me.

I saw love, tradition, purpose.
What does it mean to me to be a black woman?

When I was younger, it meant resilience. It meant unending love. It meant making everything out of what others would have called nothing. It was learning that the magician of the storybooks could not compare to that of the women in my family, the men in my family. It meant big family gatherings.

When I got older, I realized that resilience was
Often learned or rather endured. Was I strong? Or was I never allowed a moment a weakness? Was I unshakeable, or would the world look at any error as a reflection of my community and not just me.

Being black is not being able to wash away the world, because if I'm not always aware, it may One day kill me. Being black isn't choosing to be an activist, but having to be because there is no other choice but to risk your life. Being black is not being able to skip a vote, look past certain policies, or go into any workplace and not fear the secret beliefs of your peers. For me, it's about speaking up about my privilege as someone with fairer skin and much more freedoms given to me than my brothers and sisters. For me, it's having to convince people why our life is worth more than any business—because after four hundred ninety-three unarmed black people being killed by the police—it is simply more than putting a hashtag in your bio.

Being black for me is running to a protest with a mask on in the middle of a pandemic to protest the murder of an innocent black man while passing white and nonblack POC people on the street who are sitting on their boats sipping champagne, walking their dogs with their families, seeing them kayak and laugh and drink and frolic and play in the playground like Tamil rice did and live their careless lives while I'm out of breath, while my brothers and sisters can't breathe, and now I can't breathe because I can't believe I'm running through a lifestyle of people who would rather come out to Lincoln park and sit in the sun as if it was any other day. Being black is not having the privilege to be careless, to be free, or to have enough time to catch our breath.

Being black *is* magic.
But the world has convicted us of witchcraft.

Part Two:

LOVE

(The trials and tribulations of the heart)

*A look into why in the face of even the truest love
we run away from the possibility of more while gaslighting
the ones we wish to keep around most.*

Poquito Amor

You can't think.
Because thinking means that I'm not living.
Living.
Como tu.
In the present.
Con amor.
Para todos.
A heart so big it could feed a crowd—
All hungry and clawing away at the ticket man.
Admission has no limit.
No height too tall or
Too small.
Thine's love is for all.
Siempre.
No guarded cage or boarded walls.
All may enter
As long as each passerby and long stay keeps
His promise
To allow you to take the pain away.
No walls here so yours,
Mine, must fade away.
No hidden truth.
If you are to bare your sins on thine's back
Then to be naked is to be fruitful for only
Righteousness,

However no pride is present.
Prithy, tell of my sorrows and ill wishes
Upon men and women who have done me wrong.
My life had taken course.
Sin amor.
But you,
Ticket man.
Unguarded fiddle man.
Red and white striped ticket man.
At the booth of wonders with prizes,
Of sizes too colorful and too
Plentiful in numbers.
Your arms far stretched and welcoming me in.
Shards and scraps all molded into my being but you saw
Hope and potential.
Selective vision.
For you saw not my wrongs,
But wrongs done against me.
The pain pinned to my heart.
You said,
"You are not the wretched nor the wicked."
You did not falter
"No, you are sin amor."

No physical embrace but the encompassing
Love—
Warm and yellow with an auburn glow.
You glow and glow
And heal wounds without words,
Though your words do seem simple
And are often without much substance.
But ticket man,
The wonders,
Though they surround you—
Pretty plush toys,
Trinkets and puppet boys.
No ticket can tick tally's to rally up
For the greatest wonder
Of your heart.
It truly is your heart,
And what a lovely heart it is.
My ticket man
And a heart I sometimes call home.
Happy birthday.
Oh sweet
Sweet ticket man.

Love Letter To Sela

For my Sweet Sela.
You don't favor fluff or corny romantics,
But instead favor frankness on slummy afternoons because at least they're honest and
You know what to expect.
In ceramics class my sophomore year
My teacher stood at the head of the classroom and pulled out what was seemingly only a
Small ball of clay.
She stared at it and told us clay and sculpting was one of the best forms of art.
You take what is given to you and push and meld and create
Whatever you want.
It can be anything you dream it to be.
It is universal and yet so select in what it is.
You are,
In a word,
Universal.
You are to me, a mother, my grandmother, a mentor, a child, a woman
And most importantly,
One of my greatest friends.
In times of need,
Or at peoples weakest or lowest,
You hesitate none to do what has to be done.

When laughing seems almost impossible,
You, my love,
Make it look so easy.
I think that in a past life I've always wanted someone to take the world on with, to laugh at its ridiculousness.
To take one minute adventures across the city and trust because I know my girl has my back.
And I'd fight a city for you.
And yet,
Sob at where it falls short for black women like you.
You deserve the world.
I see all that you fight and I promise to you, I got you if you got me.
You are the sexy feeling a woman feels when looking at herself in the mirror.
You are the "fuck you" to every man who disrespects a woman of color.
You are the strength people need when it's time to face fears,
But also the jolting amount of laughter that fills a room after a good joke.
You are the secrets that are both bonding and sacred.
You are so sure of who you are and what you do.
You are Universal
And
You're everything I dreamed you to be.
I always got you,
Sequoia.

Love Letters In The Dark

For Ahmari.

A Small Cabin sits in the woods sits waiting.
Lake water rushing to the divide where land and consciousness
are simultaneously
Warms cusps of wind on a teary wet cheek,
Sunset beams pool into brown eyes and become new again.
For the cabin, it is neither sunset nor sunrise,
Not an ending or a beginning,
But somewhere in the middle where time and reality seem like odd
entities that are far, far away.
I am with you.
You and I.
We sit right on the dirt that once claimed us and told us we were nothing.
There we remain,
You and I.
Where our love does not end or begin,
But simply
Is.

Symphony's Sadness

For Sadie

My Eyes.
How they weep when I listen to every note
the violinist's bow lays gently in the crook of her neck.
Piano keys lightly tap in the distance.
Quiet stares so near when you think no one's paying attention
But I am.
Where is the intermission in the art of music when your mind won't stop
the symphony of sadness?
I can hear each chord, each strum, and every exhale.
How exhausted they must be.
Let them go, stop the music.
For I cannot keep up with your beauty and all its parts if I am not given
a chance.
But how is the music to stop when the conductor feels his job is
never done.
When the audiences before have never stopped and listened.
When the critic's pens are waiting to note a single fault.
But I wish to scream,
To cry with the conductor.
There are no faults in what is beauty,
What is honest,
And what is real.
Those beautiful bows and basses.
The conductor looks around and believes that art is all around.
But I have to say my dear, the most precious beauty that I see
All wrapped up within the beats of the music
Is You.

On Read

What is it about me that makes things so easy
To leave and not look back,
As if you figured out the real me—
Beyond my understanding that embraces the way you
Treated me?
Even though it left me crying
And shivering on the concrete.
Because I knew the intensity of my emotions
Would make my roommate feel uneasy.
Because you just wanted to hear how much I missed you.
Not because you actually missed me.
Why would that ever be
A factor in my reality when
All you wanted was to say you broke a
Woman like me down?
And now I'm nothing more than a
Liability—
Wanted me to open up my chest and bear
The fruit of pain you planted for the world to see
Wanted to take my tears and
Bottle them up like oil paints.
Made me record my poem on your phone for you to
Listen back to later.
Got out the car, like, "See you later,"
But your mind was already on,
Got you now.

You feel stupid.
Wow.
Talking like I'm gaslighting.
How?
But you sped off before my heart realized it confessed
To the wrong teller.
People walk out and say
Good riddance.
Keep the good in me hidden
From the rest of the world that runs to listen
About the perfect girl who's actually
Rotten on the inside.
Fatal from just one bite.
Don't bite.
She's wack anyway.
Messy girl.
Trust me, she's nothing special.
Flipping through every memory,
Every text.
All the times we made jokes about your ex
To help your pain not feel so singular.
Because you were my friend, I'd share in your grief
As if it were my own,
If only to see you smile again.
And I'll wonder where I went wrong—
Where things shifted the way I had you feeling.
For you to leave me behind,
Like it was so easy.

CM

Hey, so I thought about you today.
I saw a glimpse of the times where shakes were all but results of
our laughter.
We'd laugh and our smiles were so big because we felt like we had
each other.
I used to tell people we were going to grow old with each other, but not in
the way people think.
Our kids would have called each other "prima" and "primo."
I'd be a tia and you'd be a tio—because we must have been related or else
we wouldn't have known each other so intimately.
We must have had blood between us or else it wouldn't have felt so sure
and so real.
Crying wasn't hard- and I dreamed of the day where I could cry too.
But I didn't know the crying would be caused by you.
Those laughs turned into mean remarks.
And those smiles were nowhere to be found when I needed them most.
When they'll talk about us it'll simply be because they won't know who
abandoned who first.
You'll say it was me.
That I became a stranger and ran away and left you when I promised I
never would-

But that's just not the truth—
I left because you scared me, you scared me because you reminded me of
something I had come to fear.
And I miss you—
I miss you more than I believed I could miss a person.
But I think what hurts the most is the ringing in my ears.
The girl who looked sadly at me and said, "I can't believe he let her go."
The times I woke up sweating in the night and I turned over in my sleep
and dialed your number but you never answered—
The times you ignored me but answered her.
How it was so easy for you to let me go.
I know it's not all you—I'd be lying if I said I didn't play my part- but I
guess I thought our story never really ended and then it did.
Because somewhere deep down inside I still thought your kids would call
me tia sikoya and mine would call you tio dummy
I love you and I miss you—
I love and I miss you.
I love and I miss you.
But we're not growing old together.
We're not even together.

Hidden Feelings

I hoped one day you'd drive over. Bag for clothes to sleepover. Scary movies in your hands and face with tears like me and say you were sorry. Say you weren't going to let our friendship end. I wished you hadn't been so passive about the idea. For once I wish I wasn't the one that had to reach out to say one missed the other.

But maybe you didn't miss me.

And then the day came where I didn't think about you every couple of hours. Where time slipped and I found myself lost in the new laughter, new smiles, and new light in my eyes that I didn't think I was capable of. The feeling old folks say make them feel like kids again. Where you were too young to worry about the future and not old enough to regret your past. But in that moment of joy where you're simply present. And you finally realize the value of the gifts of today, of the people you share your days with, and you're just happy you were able to live to experience this moment, right here, without the need of validity attached to that moment.

The day came where I mourned you, the day that I resented you, and then finally the day where I just loved you. Because I was happy to have at least known you and shared such precious and intimate moments. Moments that we promised to each other. Staying up all night and dancing around the bedroom like we had two left feet. Lying in bed making stupid jokes that only we find funny.

Gifts of time with each other where all we knew was that we loved and understood each other more than anyone ever could. Moments where forever didn't seem so far away.

So I forgave you and I decided I would love you.

And now there's no room to be sad or hold tears for a once broken person or broken bond we said we'd never allow to go on. Instead days pass where I don't even think of you, where I start forgetting small details like the inside jokes we had or say things only the other would understand.

Then I forgot your birthday because I can't imagine sharing it with you anymore.

Our midnight talk sessions where we convinced each other we were licensed therapists. And after everything is gone and all the things that felt so permanent finally fade away and heal- all that will be left is love and a warm memory that I'll think of when people ask about that time in my life. Or I hear that song we always played in the car. Or I see a group of friends that reminded me of us all thinking we were grown and knowing enough to take on the world with only twenty dollars in our pocket. I'll think of those. And then I'll look down at my phone. I'll look out my window and wonder if this day is the day you drive over. And then I'll smile and remember we're not in that chapter of our lives anymore. And I'll send love and light your way.

Love Poem

What is empty space but a blank canvas?
Pushing at the clunk and the junk and the
Things that never belonged.
What's a broken heart but a person who desired for the idea of love,
But never had it?
And what am I but a girl who wishes to give you the world if only to see
hope for the realization of an idea,
Reflected in a wide mouth of lovely pearls and to not constantly
wonder if the words and the phrases that loose from lips when ears are
folded down?
Won't one day fall upon one deaf and one sound.
It is here that I see,
That in this interwoven timeline between you and me,
That in the intermission of my life and a break in between chapters,
That a new beginning blossoms in a place that I once called purgatory.
You say you're spiritual now,
Well I am too.
But for some reason when I ask the stars at night that shine in your eyes
so bright,
I have no clue what to do.
Where prophecies on old scrolls guarantee an outcome,
And the whispers of our ancestors guided us on beaten paths,
Paved before the days we were born.
But even completely lost and left unanswered by the skies,
I'm happy and overjoyed to know that
The unknown has become a home for
You and I.

And so I won't wait,
And I won't wither,
Drowning in the ocean of myself conscious
That tries to bring sense and reason into why our stories have
become tethered.
I only know the warmth from the fire
Burning in my cheeks when you look at me the way that you do,
Or the plush feel of your lips against mine,
Or the craving for your touch,
That feels like Pillsbury cookies and eggnog
On Christmas morning,
Like home.
And so I'll stay there,
Well rested and coddled up,
And in no rush to move forwards or backwards,
Or anywhere in between,
I'll wrap myself up in what I know to be you,
And free my mind of any dream of what is
To come for the both of us.
Because my dear,
You were not gifted to me in a passing fantasy of tomorrow.
But rather,
The blissful unpredictability of today.
And for me sweet K,
That will always be okay,
Love yours truly,
Sequoia

Easy Cuz' You're Beautiful

Loving you.
I'll always remember the nights we had
Treasure you.
You'll always have a special place in my heart.
Grounded by you.
You have such a sense of grounding people.
Perfect listener.
You always know exactly what to say.
Trained mentor.
You've pushed me to be a better person.
Thank you.
But I never signed up to be the special world in
Your Hero's Journey,
For you to slip in and take all the magic
And slip out when you were ready to return
Back to a reality that didn't include me in it.
Because that was so much more comfortable.
It had so much less accountability.
I'll always be a good friend to you,
But you were never a good friend to me.
Waiting anxiously,
Life has gotten to be
Warm and just right.
I gave you my light so that the undiscovered you
Could come crawling out from the dark.
Inspired you.
Now you know who you want to be.
Don't thank me or tell me you'll always have
A special place in your heart for me.
Don't tell me you'll
Treasure the time we once had
While digging my grave you once inhabited.
Stop telling me I changed your life
I'm trying to forget how you changed mine.

Soggy Sweatshirt

We were moving in the rain.
It was drizzling and I was
Shivering,
But I was wearing the hoodie you told me
Was your favorite.
I was sad this day.
Not sad because I was moving,
But sad because I felt like I finally became
Part of the cycling attraction show.
That was my surroundings.
That was like the warning signs and the
Never ending loop
They teach you about in health class.
The hoodie smelled like you,
The way that you do.
It made me smile,
And I felt safe.
I know we haven't known each other long,
But I feel like I've known you forever—
Can I know you forever.
I feel like I'll always know you,
Even if your time will expire knowing me
Forever.

Clear Skies

I was at the park with my dog
When I thought of you.
The wide open sky
And encompassing dark blue.
I saw all the stars and began to wonder
What evening spell had you put me under
To lay on my back and watch the clouds pass
The moon and its light that began to dance
In my thoughts that held each memory and hue
Like planets that formed galaxies all
Dedicated to you,
As rare as the Little Dipper,
And as frequent as a shooting star.
Endless bliss with your spiritual company
Makes me think eternity can't be that far
To take on this life with you.
A beaten path that had not started with two
Like a story book magic moment.
As I look into the night sky,
I can only come to hope
There's a future for you and I.

When My Loneliness Begets Sadness

What happens when my loneliness meets my sadness
And their interactions lead to madness,
Telling me lies about how I fell for you?
When falling for you was never a part of the overview,
But just a burning flame that was meant to be.
Put out.
I don't want to put you out,
But the idea of you fooling me into you truly
Being
The only one I need
Now has my mind filled with doubt.
Wishing you disclosed the information
That these sheets wouldn't be.
That I wouldn't be
The first host that it's taken.
I guess I'm mistaken.
Painted you as the perfect you.
You
Told me I should have never doubted you
Because Good guys
Tell greats lies.
When all they want is the idea of you.
The completion of two.
The creak of the bedspring to remind you you're still living
But never breathing

Any breath of life but taking what you feel.
Only I can give you.
I give you
Every moment and every crumb of time I reserve for myself.
Set a seat at the table
Of my being.
In between the side dishes
And the side bitches,
And taking up the space where self-love and self-preservation were my
main guests,
And are now nowhere in attendance.
Because your needs and my want
To please
Have become a permanent resident.
I know you don't mean for
Your needs to take precedence.
Maybe I brought this on.
Perhaps I shifted the lenses in my eyes
Like the picture movies we bought as kids,
Clicking past each frame until
I projected onto you.
All the promises daddy could never fill.
Maybe you and I were never real,
Feeling like you were never mine to steal.
Give you back to the girl who spoke
Words onto me like she was a queen

And I was the other woman.
But I'm not the other woman.
I'm a woman.
A woman you'll never see
Fulfill your every prophecy
Of perfect bedroom harmonies.
Singing your notes eloquently
And screaming your name in bold letters
For the world to see.
I think you said it perfectly,
That my worry would manifest into anger and that anger would carry
me to
New heights
Like a hot air balloon—
Too high to not realize how
Small of a man you really are.
But in those moments
When my toes won't touch the ground
Because it's shaken from all that
You've taken from me,
I see your face in my mind.
A padded blindfold against my eyes.
And suddenly a justified reason to completely hate you,
I cannot find,
Because your lips were once mine,
And the lines in your palm were once storylines that I was a part of,

And this air that's become my fare
On trip a to nowhere but here.
To see you for you
Used to be a eulogy to a past broken soul that sought refuge in you.
And you opened your arms wide for me
Taking up space you knew you could not
Lease out.
And so that part of me that hates you
Can't help but understand you.
And know that perfect people don't exist.
And neither do perfect coincidences.
And now you got me here reminiscing
What happens when my loneliness begets my sadness
And manifests into this madness
Where I hate you.
But I need you.
And all I want is to feel you.
But scared that I'm past the point of wanting this.
Because I've gotten too good at being with just me.
You pulled back the curtain and I saw my own reflection
And I realize you never deserved my affection,
Not even a fragment of my attention.
But I gave it freely
And I guess I now know the real me.
The me that gives too much unintentionally.
But aye,
I guess it's what it be.

Sizzurp

Drink of my libations
Recite back to me my every cantation
That I sang onto your body while you slept
And I crept into your sacred sheets.
See me for the real me
And don't snag your lips on what you want to see,
Like a fantasy you keep on passing me
For an undersold rotten canopy.
Speak out from the rainwater
And wrap your ribbons on my rusted kettle spoon.
Rift in my tides for this sudden swoon.
Fill my mind with your parallels that you saw in yesterday's moon.
Don't praise me like a deity
And forsake the raven works inside of me
That twist and turn like the buttermilk at a party with my family.
And I promise I won't grow tired,
Weak from bottled up envy hoping you'd admire
The way my eyes saunter and dance around your
Words,
As if they were actually interesting.
As if they fueled some type of star crossed fire.

From Mine

I know you got a heart apart from mine,
Seeking for sanctity in the divine
But blinded to the new course I find in thine's
Breath and hums between whimpers.
I know that you
Don't see why I'm hurt
For you.
It's only a time scattered in frequencies you believed
Would never reach my ears.
What do I see in your loving
But bottled up fears
And in these mirrored tears
Viewed through paper thin glass.
I see you pull her deeper.
I realize I'm the student and the not teacher.
The other woman.

Just Tell Me

Don't let the pitter patter of the rain outside
Be so loud you can't hear my whispers to your heart.
Why do you sit so far away from me on that windowsill?
Come closer.
Won't you tell me about your walks in Morocco.
The post cards you sent home but got lost in transit.
Oh remember our ventures to Milan,
Through the scope of your bedroom walls and
The posters
We'd tear out of books in the travel section.
The smell of strawberries and cream coming from the Eiffel Tower on
your ceiling.
Don't cry dear.
You'll only wipe away all that I painted on your skin with my lips.
I'll paint them again.
Vous êtes si belle.
As you sleep,
Wrapped tightly in your arms,
I'll trace the lines in your face that split into my favorite parts of you.
Where the skin raises and curves
Into those lips that seduce me back into bed when
I promise to depart.
Embraces-moi fort avant de partir.
Listen.
Can you hear the postman down stairs ringing the bell?
I thought the mail didn't come today.
Isn't it Sunday?
No. Don't. It can wait

For now. I'll take you in bit by bit
To the tempo of the rain outside.
Do you still want for me in the moments your mind melts into empty
time and space?
Kiss me darling.
I'm afraid if I go another minute without you pressed against me I might
Give into my fate and slip into the night for the final time
With feathered brows raising at the tattered hems of my pantyline,
Torn off in a hurry but
Gingerly did the hands move to caress my thighs.
You knew what you were doing to me.
How musical you became,
Flicking your every finger.
Stroking me into a crescendo and redefining my every movement.
Write me into your manifesto
Please.
Let me fall helplessly into your arms.
May the words bleed onto white scrolls.
May every stroke push deeper and edge closer
As the trembles of my inner thighs release and steady.
Won't you hold me only for one more moment?
Won't you let me become your life's work?
Won't you take my body and tune its every inch to the music in
your mind
That won't play for ears untouched by your words?
Come closer my dear.
I think the mailman has rung for you again.
I think he hears us,
Oh but who cares.

I'll play until the wood splits and the reed cracks in my mouth.
I'll belt out the notes you envisioned in my nakedness,
And I'll succumb to your whims and the music created between
our connection,
Spattered all over the cotton sheets and pillows wrinkled from my pull.
But if for one second
You find your eyes lost within the music and not within the
Silent Solos I let synthesize between the rise and fall of my chest,
Trailing the curve in my neck and widening of my mouth.
Were you to play the notes inscribed on my breasts but never finish the
full measure in my eyes,
If I rest too long.
Sing into me your truth and never anything woven in the night and not
By candle light.
Call out to me during your sail away.
Nowhere near
The port in my tenderness and everlasting desire for our own scores.
If for even one moment you feel the beats begin to lag behind
Our given tempo,
Tell me,
For I cannot live to see the day where the seat beside me lays cold
And my head shall sway to a musical love affair
In an auditorium where the attendance is one
And the instruments have all been transported elsewhere,
Blind to the new absence
And now dancing to a tune that no longer exists,
For a conductor that has gone on to play for other ears.
Oh won't you just come a little closer,
My dear.

A Lover's Kiss

I long for my lover's kiss,
The way the senses danced between our lips,
Like time and its promise to expire
Had become a concept you could
Choose not to believe.
In between the single inhale and the closeness of our
Heavy breathing,
A home strung addict to this feeling
But that pull from me to you had not been
A feeling
New to you.
For she had only taken the same steps as
She threw her head back and let herself fall
Victim
To a man who pretended to be
All that she needed.
And for me, I cannot follow suit
Because she is woman
And a woman in which I now know
Every press I make against you.
I hear the soft pleas of my sister
That whither and break at the bond I thought
You and I had.
For when I reached for your forearm above me while we painted and
hung a tapestry
In my memory

Of our bodies melting into the oil paints,
That sleek touch,
The soft cries seducing you back into my rhythm now faint
As our hips moved and sank into each other,
I reach for your forearm
But I grab where her hand was instead.
Where the Symphony of colors played between
Beats
And drums
Of her Hums.
The hues of blue that dotted the last
Q of your mosaic of play things.
And feel goods so that you
Don't have to be the bad guy.
Eyes wide.
Soul sisters.
But never knowing each other's names.
But I know her touch,
And I know her gaze,
And her taste that still lingers on your skin.
Circling my breast like you were foreign to the idea
Of love.

A Vu

Amor pequena.
Amor de mis sueños.
Stuffed between the cracks of the textile ceiling,
A charitable sun breaks the sweat on my cheek.
A kiss on my neck
There in the middle of ivory square where we first meet.
Colliding and causing my foot to slip there
Under your claustrophobic steps.
Like the sweet juice of an overripe plum, I drank of you—
Saw you in the milk of the sea—
Allure in smell like the wood smoking beneath the stove.
Margarita.
It burns there too.

My Wish

My mind and body could never agree on all the things I'd want to say.
How can you decide when there's more than one form of communication
Through my body which you've made a vessel for the things you wish
buried forever,
In my veins that you pumped with lead?
Shall I run up to her on sight and pull her in for a loving embrace?
Shall I let my lips divulge in all the ways I've come to know her through
my own experience?
How my love and understanding took
Greater leaps
And found tragic falls in the holes in my
Patience
And character
That I hadn't known were still there?
Hidden behind the trauma and denial to
Truth
I had become so accustomed to.
How shall I greet the one I call
Soul sister,
When she not know even my presence
In her life,
Or her past that she wished to never revisit.
I excuse her actions,
Look past her harbored malice for me because
I know that the hollowness can
Swallow you whole.
To be in love with someone who once shared
In your embrace,
But found interest in someone else's young face.

Must I pretend I do not care for her deeply
When I do,
Because I have grown an understanding for the bond
Between you two?
And though it keeps me up at night,
The thought that she will never fold
In the fight for your affection and validation,
Yet
Hesitation meets my quickness to call
Home wrecker,
Or cheap thrill,
When unkept emotional storage
Had become your responsibility to fill.
But she was left high and dry
With glazed eyes and a question mark at the box marked
The great love of my life.
She projected onto you the fullness she could never feel at home.
I plead guilty on the stand for sharing sorrow
For the one who couldn't see me go
Faster than I ever came into the picture,
A fixture in her mind of the
Perfectly painted
Portrait of your coming together—
A union not made in secrecy or privacy but
Plastered on every billboard and photograph.
Posted on illuminated screens for all to see.
The slouch in her arms and the way she looked
Not at me,
But into me,
Like I had been the final plunge in her already
Crisp paper heart.

The one you tore at like an impatient child.
To break things you find too untouched by
Your chaos.
Your words after
Six months of one day,
Someday but not today,
Because saying you want only one person
Would be to you
A thorn in your tender heel.
A modern day Achilles with
A weakness.
Feelings of immediate death
When trying to loosen the noose that is the
Possibility of forever.
But to you.
To you
Was never supposed to stretch thinner than
Your promise
Of only momentary
Sensory pleasure.
I weep for her while I lay next to you,
Realizing that one day our distance will be
Closed.
Our stories
Will merge into one big narrative
Of all the women you diminished into
Schoolgirls who's daddies didn't show up
For the big class recital.
And I'll belt out the notes of my solo
Into the microphone for all those around to know
I practiced, so that native ears could
Meet my work,
Time,
And efforts
With praising cheers.

The empty chair that creaked from the weight
Of hope in her heart
But acceptance that this was how things were.
She deserves to know that
She wasn't the one showing up short
At the card game of turmoil you brought her to,
Where you dangled monogamy on the table
Like a full house wasn't dancing at your fingertips.
And your prize
Was more time
To pull from her all that you wanted out of a relationship.
Without your signature,
Without your consign to a concept that she could defend in court,
Were you not to live up to standard
I cannot simply let her go on without her knowing
You were never the man fit enough to indulge in her presence.
Her stride was meant for your neck
To break beneath her heel,
Not follow the path into your bed sheets.
I must sing to her a tune for spirituality,
To cleanse her aura
And reinstate her peace.
Tell her that I'm learning to love me through her
Trials,
And her brokenness.
And in her shattered flesh
Like windows in an old church
I found
Bandages for my wounds
That cut deep beneath my breast and rib cage.
I see her art
And wished for her that the soft tip of her
Paint brush
Never stroked along the white lines of your
Inconsistency and toxic male ego

A need to be different from the rest but
Never feeling like those red flags
Are simply lessons my fellow sisters wanted to pass on to me.
My heart thirsts for a companion.
In her I see fit
A chance to let a fellow soul know that
She is seen.
She is heard.
And the hurt that she still carries
I've offered my back to carry for only a moment,
So that she may once again reclaim the rest you
Stole from her bedside.
And in time
I call on her to weep with me
In the tunnel I can see so
Distantly.
When these soul sisters
Have become babysitters
On the playground of your wrongdoing,
And I'll intent
Our harmonies served on a silver dish.
For the full disclosure to my soul sister
Is the secret deed
To carry it out
Is my only wish.

Pink Scrunchie

I don't think you'll ever fully know how loving you has tested my heart—
Tested my patience.
And how I wish it weren't so hard for you to want me.
Because I want you
Entirely.
You keep talking about other women and you have me
Going through your Twitter likes to see that you've liked other women.
And now I realize maybe you'll never be satisfied
With standing by my side.
As if the role was too belittling.
When I kiss you, I feel our paths melting into one that we can
Walk together.
Your hands are bruised and broken from pulling them apart
Again
And again.
And leaving me to wonder if the words you spoke into my heart were
built upon living in the moment or me loving the way you looked at me.
Because no one had ever looked at me like I was important.
Like the things I thought in my mind were painted together with
pure genius.
Loving you is draining.
I fall in love everyday
With your smile and the way you laugh at my jokes
That were never funny.

But after seeing the girls you keep calling honey,
I'm starting to think that the punchline of the
Ongoing joke that made you erupt with laughter
Was me.
And now I'm sinking down in my chair afraid to realize that we were
soulmates who crossed paths too soon.
I'm speeding down I-90 and I can't wait for you to catch up.
Don't want to teach you that this tempo can't be compared to other sheet
music that had a different ensemble than the one I see play into the night
as you hold me close.
You say I'm indifferent but that's
Not true.
I'm just simply accepting the heartbreak before it happens.
Because to fight what you've already begun in my
Mind
Is fruitless.
You're wearing my pink scrunchie as you sing to me loudly.
But then why are your affirmations to our union in the tone of whispers?
It's unfinished—
My feelings for you and my words.

Blue Light

Heavenly Father.
I know we haven't spoken in a while.
And maybe you're disappointed in me for doing those things
And I guess I've avoided our talks because I've been ashamed of what you
might think of me,
Things have been kinda hard lately.
I've been feeling really down.
And my heart keeps breaking more than I knew it could.
And the sinking feeling in my chest won't seem to go away.
I'll be smiling at work and laughing with friends,
But the feeling will still be there,
And I'll think to myself,
Why can't I just be happy?
And I just know people are getting tired of me.
I just don't want to ruin something great because I'm sad
Or because I feel like I don't deserve it.
If there's some bad energy I let walk into my life
Or there's something I spoke over myself, Father,
I pray that you bless me.
And that you take it off of me.
Please.
Please just take it off of me.
Please.
It would mean so much to me.
I know it's probably a part of the journey.
But can I take a break.
I just need to catch my breath.
If not,
Then I pray my loved ones never feel the burden
Of my shattering heart.
May they go on with their lives without notice
Of my sinking eyes.
I pray I get better.
I pray I get better.
Amen

What Brings You comfort?

My love is like an open account.
Bank teller says there's an overcharge.
How can your heart begin to weave its flesh
Back to seamlessness
From a hurt when you're still not the first choice
And you're the only option?
How do you come second to yourself?
You give permission.
How can the right person always be at the wrong time but in the right
chapter of your life?
Perfection is such an endless tease.
Dirty slut.

Friends 'Til The End

Hi.
Are we friends?
Let's hang out and dance till the end.
Be my light.
Tickle my tummy with laughter and joy.
Independent.
We're so independent.
All we need is each other and the
Home we've created.
I'll hold your hand and come over
When I know you're sad and need empty space
To not feel so
Encompassing.
I'm only a phone call away.
My papers will be pushed
Away, away, and away,
So that time can tick like collecting stones
And not tick down like a ticking time bomb—
Exploding and leaving you void of understanding,
Instead of just a summary for you to examine
Later in your head but never to my lips.
Or ears.
Or heart.
You're my best friend,
My one true best friend,
Til the end.
The end.
I'm sorry, maybe later.
My lover called out my name and I must
Retreat.
God, why are you being so needy?
Yeah that must suck.

Hey can we talk later?
I can't that day I'm busy.
Pictures of sceneries unknown plaster my screen.
Friends?
You're my best friend.
I already have plans. I'll let you know when I'm
Not busy.
I'll always be here.
Wanna go to the movies and just sit there?
Give me your attention because I know
It'll always be there.
My lover and I —
We're in a quarrel.
Let's sit and talk about morals
Like we used to do and not look at the clock.
All I need is us
Back to normal.
Oh, he called me.
It's all a new.
I'm busy, I thought you knew.
We're grownups now. I don't have time.
There's greater things on the line.
You know I'm bad with texting.
Stop forcing me to love you.
I love you.
That void I can never fill—
Fix it yourself.
Just fix it yourself.
Of course we're friends.
We'll be friends forever.

Palabras de Azul

You asked me what was on my mind.
I obliged.
The dirty burgundy confession box in my mind.
I allowed you the time.
Lied and said I was fine.
Until you told me I had one chance to tell you the truth
Or else you didn't wanna hear it.
I unloaded onto you only a
Fraction
Of the things that had become an overbearing
Distraction in my day to day life.
I asked for one thing.
A complete reaction since it was on the phone
Hundreds of miles away from reach
In a city that had everything you wanted and
Not me.
But you didn't answer.
You left my mouth open with insecurity still dripping
From my lips.
Memories of you grabbing onto my hips
As our energies peaked and mangled each other
Until becoming one.
I have nothing to say.
Are you kidding me?
You're left speechless and overwhelmed. Well, guess
How I feel?
I can't believe this is real.
I'm begging a man to want me in the span of time it took me to
Love him.
Fuck him.
I've realized you don't know what you want.
But I know what I desire.
To stop feeling this way.
Because, Nigga, I'm tired.

Let Go

I felt my chest rise and fall.
It's speed pumping fear into my veins
For the idea that it may never stop,
May never cease,
And that my heart may finally give out after this
Final blow.
I listened to the same words over and over again.
You told me,
"I just don't want to be with you,"
And I wondered how your feelings could vanish for me
In what was only twenty-four hours.
In what was once a plea to not let go of something
That didn't come to us so easily with others.
I felt myself becoming the person
I promised I'd never one day become.
And sounding too desperate to care what
A past me would think of who I now am,
If that meant keeping you.
I love you.
But you're not willing to suffer through it with me.
I can't convince you to want me.
I held onto my chest
And whispered to myself to let go,
To please let go.
You were done.
And my heart had been tested for the final time.

Love Capacity

Why is it so hard for us to love one another?
Feel intensely and know that those emotions are special?
To desire and protect something so much?
How could that be so wrong?
Why is it that
I need to love you for months
To know I love you eternally?
I need to find something wrong with you.
Pick apart each conversation until you slip up
And think if that fault will manifest,
Or earn my loving.
But I don't withhold my love for a probation period.
From the moment our eyes meet,
Our energies,
Kismet,
I love you.
Why are we so afraid to love?
Time is man-made.
The ethereal energy that is
Love
is bound by the universe.
And she does not own a clock.
So then why would I?

Skeema Scamma

Infiltrate my mind with your eyes
And tell me I remind you of something divine.
That I've managed to pick apart your time
And take what I know is already mine.
Call out my name in the summer's night.
Scream from the rooftops—
Ma ama my mood is a lota
Topsy turvey, if you know what I mean.
Let's take our clothes off and run a mile.
Rub dirt on my body like you see a muse
In my nudity.
Co-conspirator in my self-depletion.
It's my aroma that's got you fiending
For physical touch and emotional healing.
Where's yo daddy at, scary boy?
Treating this dynamic like it's a toy.
Conjure up the algorithms
Or mold my cantations into
Prosperous manifestations.
And call me Congo,
Cuz I'm rich with your fruit, baby
Just let me know.

Coveted Bed Sheets

I thought that maybe the act between you and I
Would somehow blind my open eyes.
Infect my stable mind
From seeing any future mistakes.
Or in fear that my heart might break
From knowing I chose the wrong one.
Or maybe I'd begin to bend to your every whim
Every "compromise" that was really a one way street
That only lead to your insatiable desire for watered down ego.
If only to give justification for why I let you in.
But no.
If anything now I loathe you.
I despise the very faux helpless look.
The wanting to be good guy persona that you just won't shed.
And now I understand I never had to worry about your ex
If I were to finally rid you of my life,
What a life that might be.
To be centered around only me.
I'd never look back either,
Only pity the next girl who thought she was "different."
I'm glad it all transpired
Because only now I realize it was never your body I was meant to admire,
Destined to desire.
It was mine

I Think I Saw You Today

I think I saw you today.
In a moment I thought it was her.
A woman just like you.
I took the call and heard you in her voice,
In the way that I rejoiced,
In the way I could see you again and hope that
Today amongst the days that had passed would reach out
And loved me in the way that I had always loved you.
With my heart fully open and ready to forgive because
I had healed.
Rejoiced in my meals and only hoped you had done the same.
Didn't listen to the words that the two had said,
Because even you had admitted I was the only one who didn't make you
Feel dread.
Because I never body shamed when I was with you.
They loved you but spoke about how other women
Were built.
How that made them ugly,
But loved you with all their heart and never realized the weight of
their words.
And even now here I was
Ready to welcome you back with open arms.
And then she arrived.

She wasn't you but looked just like you in older age.
In the same demeanor and smile.
In the way we rejoiced together for miles on the train rides to Julian's.
When you saw the only clawing at my own pockets when I could barely
afford a thing.
How I always made the best of what I had and tried to surround you in
the love languages I knew.
When she left, I almost cried because she was you.
But she didn't recognize.
How could she?
How could she?
When in the end you didn't even recognize me,
Couldn't love me beyond what the group said.
Because "sanctuary" was supposed to be that.
But now as I come back to this poem I realize I was the reason
people wanted
To come over.
But my love for you all overshadowed the ways in which
You spread inner security.
Because I thought being around you all made you better as you made me.
But maybe I was wrong,
Because as others began to love me.
You all began to resent me.

Began to hate the love I showed to other people.
Began to feel insecure in what you know and when our friend came to me
And told me the horrible things being said.
I didn't want to believe it,
Because you all loved me.
You all had to have loved me.
You had to have loved me.
So that night I called out your name and hoped you would hear,
Both in my trembling and in my tears.
The way my heart broke on the concrete I fell on.
The way Leah picked me up as I fell.
And even as she filled me with love
How could I believe that?
When I had told some of those I thought loved me the most
That I had heard death in my toast to truth for years.
How you allowed time to drift after I showed my love and you
withheld yours.
I still love you.
But I see now, it was never me.
But as you told me that night,
I'm not all that innocent.

Butt Hurt Baby

I keep replaying in my head the things you said to me.
Confidently.
Without worrying about you.
Hurting me.
I can't believe
You said you think I like you more than you like me,
Like I must be sitting up going crazy
Imagining scenarios programmed into my mind.
Don't call me baby.
In the morning when you realized I reclaimed my time.
Reclaimed my favor.
Stop doling out harshness like you're doing me a
Fucking favor.
Post that bitch one more time.
You act like reassurance and transparency requires
All your leftover labor.
You know
You called me with a smirk on your face,
Just trying to erase
The fact that you left me on the phone with half a heart.
Stolen art.

Bamboozled self-image in which I took part
To give you this cockiness you hang off your belt.
New found strut and these bitches start to melt.
They all up in ya face,
Reversing the roles in you and I's chase.
Making me feel like these past couple months
Have been a waste.
I hesitate
To say that there's no chance
For you and I to resurge our romance
To when it was pure and honest,
And keeping your attention didn't feel like a contest.
Country style pig
Wearing my blue ribbon.
Winning top two for your eyes.
That is the prize.
I'll get in where I fit in.
I refuse to fail to mention
The way your tongue swayed in your mouth
When you injected into my being self-doubt,
Like it wasn't my name you couldn't wait to get out.
In these streets,
Like you bagged a dime.

Too bad I didn't attach a fine to my time,
Had you come up short on what's yours and what's mine.
I shoulda seen the signs
When you hung up on me to talk to your ex.
And the last time y'all spoke is when you both were
Having sex.
I already know the rest.
It was just a fling.
It's not what we got,
Cuz baby we got the real thing.
This shit really stings.
To feel like you're not valid,
Not important,
Not nearly held to value.
I ignored all the bullshit
Feeling like I had to.
But there's no mistakes.
Only lessons
In this crime, baby.
You'll be prosecuted
As a felon.
And my time I spend without you.
As far as sentence time,
There is no telling.

I may go days,
Or even weeks
For our next exchange. I will not
Be the first to speak,
The first to laugh.
The first to light fire to gas
You poured onto me,
Hoping I'd ignite,
So I'd feel bad about starting another fight.
But I'm cool.
You not about to make me look like a fool.
Since you wanted time,
Baby you got it.
I'll bottle up my feelings for you
In a bottle rocket
And send them off to the moon for the
Craters to hold.
And I won't revisit them again.
I wanted to fall in love with a friend
And hoped it would never end.
But it did before it even began.
Just wanted you to be my man,
Not only cater to your fans.
Girls who knew I was temporary
While you told me stories of us one day married.
This whole experience has just been very
Draining.

Tethered to this Timeline

Why do we stick around for so long?
Tell ourselves it'll get better?
He'll start doing the things he promised.
Listen to my words and carry them in the pupils of his eyes
As he brings my wishes for better suited intimacy
Into fruition.
An unnatural relation to our inner nature,
Trying to forge some form of explanation
As to why he's worth the wait—
Worth providing an escape
For his crumbling bricks and cracked asphalt.
Why do we treat love like an investment and not an experience
That's supposed to radiate with only the highest of energies.
Colored sapphire
Burning coals in our hearts and not sands under our
Feet,
Made for us to walk across for a lover who won't even
Claim us.
Why do we gift our time in the prettiest of bows in the form of
Complacency,
Saying simplistic suitors can be tutored to
Dress us of the worth they don't believe we've earned yet?

Am I crazy for wondering why you don't want me after four months
of waiting?
Four months of contemplating if you ever wanted more.
Now revising my writing so now it's
Eight months.
Wondering some more as you slip on the floor you lathered
With your slippery tongue and want for fun,
In process of making me look dumb.
Wasted my light on the stone pinching future
You called bright.
Why do we give so much and accept so little?
Leaving our boundaries we spent years building in
The middle
And wondering why the bedside still feels cold
With blankets of empty words he's sewn into your seams.
Why do we wait it out
When they haven't even shown us something
Worth waiting for?
I'm done being tethered to this endless timeline.
I've found the key to my true bliss
And it's outside this door.
Why would I wait for more?

Me Over You

Love shouldn't feel this way.
Uneasy at every turn.
Worried that you'll stumble into the girl meant for you.
Because we're only dating.
Because I'm not your girl yet.
While I drive on the expressway and save my
Tips for gas
To sleep next to you because we keep each other
Warm at night.
But I'm not your girl yet.
Because we talk everyday
And you tell me about how I make you feel
Complete.
But it still don't feel right.
You don't want only me.
You need to be sure.
Okay.
But I can't do this anymore.

I'm so tired of feeling in competition with someone
Not in the picture yet.
I'm tired of feeling like the intermission girl,
Not the sunset girl.
Like the future bitter ex girl.
Honey, I'm exhausted.
Are you not calling because you're bored
Or because some girl at the club finally said yes?
Because I'm not your girl yet,
And you are still posting paintings from your ex.
Why don't you wanna love me
The way I wanna love you?
I'm not your girl yet,
So then let me go.
I'm sorry,
But I don't recognize me anymore.
And it's been months,
And it still don't feel right.

Work

Every call seems so much more distant.
Every message left unread.
I thought you told me you missed me.
Then why does it feel like you're waiting for me to leave?
You say you'll see me eventually.
That's why you're not pressed to make it now.
This is starting to feel so much like work,
And you're burning the time until you go out of town.
I'd stay up late and drive over just to be by your side,
But you could go another two months without me,
As long as you know you're the only thing plaguing my mind.
You're devaluing my time
And all the energy I can't stop putting in.
If you wanted to see me, you'd find a way.
If you missed me there'd be more things to say
Than the same dried out small talk you provide me as a filler.
I'm not ashamed to admit I'm sad
And I'm realizing you might not be worth it.

Fool's Gold

I felt like I had grown to know you.
Grown to expect every twist and turn.
Know that you loved me but
You just needed time to give it a voice to fill.
I thought I managed enough to keep you thrilled with my presence.
Treat it like a present you get to enjoy in the present.
But even as I made home in the creases of your mouth
As you smiled,
I still couldn't quiet the ringing in my ears once you said her name.
Another Woman.

Frida's Trolley

When I look back at these months,
How they escaped my breath when I came to speak of them.
The moments of feeling like we were holding on
Desperately to an idea of forever.
Dancing in a living room not yet lived in.
Pleading for joy to become effortless,
A desire for springtime in the time of baren fruit.
I remember how the soil turned rot beneath our palms.
It was like running so fast.
Trying to make it to the finish line before my feet could make the feat.
The wind breaking across my face.
The accidents in my life are few,
But none compare to the day I decided to love you.
I remember your tears watering me—
Thinking they would help me bloom.
But I only wilted.
Sunlight escaping my view.
The accidents in my life are not many,
But none come close to the day I promised to trust you.

Table for Two

I wish we could've meet
At the coffee shop with peanut butter toast with glazed banana slices and
a drizzle of honey.
We'd get coffees or hot chocolate and spend the first few moments
catching up.
I wish we could have sat down together as friends
Because in another life that's what we would have been.
Or maybe sisters hiding beneath sheets with the flashlight telling
scary stories
Where our biggest fears were monsters hiding beneath our beds.
Not in them, holding us close while we slept.
Maybe we would have meet at Girl Scout camp,
Running around looking for thistles and rocks to make
Mud pies out of.
Making dream catchers by the river bank and
Splitting a peanut butter and jelly sandwich as we rested.
I'd let you have my pudding cup, because I'd lie and say I didn't want it,
Because I knew how it would make you smile.
I think we would have been the two little girls tied to the hip, maybe
Sitting too close at the bonfire
With our marshmallows already burnt to a crisp
But too caught up in the laughter from the day
That we forgot to see the stars of the night.

In another life we would have shared laughter instead of tears
And hopes for each other instead of our fears.
I wish we could've sat down together as friends.
Talked about what happened to us both,
Like we were leading ladies in our own sitcoms.
Like Sex in the City.
Or Living Single.
And we'd realize that we knew each other too well
To ever raise our tongues against one another.
I wish you knew why I did what I did.
Why I closed that door.
Or why I knew you would hate me in the end.
But I did it anyway because I thought I was only looking out for you the
way no one had ever looked out for me.
I wish you knew my heart and knew me until now,
And why everything you said about me wasn't true.
Why the words you said hurt me so much.
I wish we could've known each other.
Because in another life we were sisters.
I think maybe we could have been friends.
Girl Scouts.
Admiring each other's reflection on the surface of the river bend.

Pick Up

I feel so defeated.
I don't really know what to even say.
I guess that you really broke my heart,
And all you did was tell me the truth.
That I gave my all
When you gave me nothing.

How Can I?

How is it that I can lay next to you?
Be there when you turn and look into my eyes.
Have your skin pressed against mine while we
Wait for the other to speak.
How can I be only inches away from you
And feel completely and utterly alone?

Nightstand

At the break of dawn you slipped away from me,
When my skin turned a sweet marmalade
Behind the shutters that were open.
Eyes feathered close.
Long strokes of bed rest on my cheek.
The springs didn't even creek
In fear that they might give you away.
It was never your desire to stay.
You slipped a crinkled note on my nightstand,
One that you kneaded in the palm of your hand as if it'd
Melt into you
Like a grainy tattoo for me to read.
For your lips to later relay to my ears.
Nipples taunt under the cotton,
Passing your hand one final time,
Only to pull the clasp of your silver chain.
But then you paused
To let your eyes replay in your mind
Every liquid silk fault you had grown to once love.
Fixating on my hips
Angled towards you with an open hand,
But no urgency to feed
My insatiable thirst for your special type of intimacy.
But you wouldn't linger for much longer
Because your eyes didn't narrow into mine.
Your fingertips didn't dance or run along the lines in my palm.
Rather, they wished to tighten around my hips.
Speak absurdity on my lips
And leave me once again
Broken and restless.
You didn't love me.
You never did.

Say it to Me

Stop writing it down for me to read later.
Or hanging up when it's your turn.
Stop asking me what's wrong when I've poured out
Every answer.
I'm tired of guessing.
Tell me how you feel,
How you think of me or feel for me—
Want for me and deject the very feeling of loss.
Say to me what I say to you
Endlessly,
Which is in the way I hope you would undress me of my emotions
And give me momentary devotions
That I give to you endlessly.
Please just look at me.
Say it to me.
How I look.
How I feel.
Because none of this feels real anymore.

Spoiled Ricotta

I imagine us fighting sometimes
In my room or yours.
Saying all the things I wish I could in a feat of anger.
Screaming and crying and breaking things that don't feel like mine.
Appearing to me in broken images like a skipping film strip.
I'm saying all the things I usually let fizzle out after the initial fire
When I'm already too tired
And too ready to release these feelings to even be bothered with knowing
what to do with it all.
I'm throwing glasses, cups, books.
All painted the same color—even the pages.
Red, blue, and sometimes yellow.
And I'm one hundred percent.
Absolutely.
Undoubtedly.
Rattled to my core.
Sometimes I'm crying so hard my face bunches up like a sun-dried raisin.
Sometimes I'm crying so hard I don't even make a sound.
My elbows tuck into my side.
My arms fold in on each other.
My knees are growing weaker.
And I'm falling,
But you're nowhere near to catch me.
You're on the other side of the bed.
Your face is out of view.
And your hands are swaying at your sides.
Sometimes I'm just mad.
Angry at whatever you've done now,
And you can hear the rage in my voice and in my tone.

I'm so mad you probably don't recognize me.
But I do.
Whenever I imagine these things,
I always see myself.
See how it would look like if I ever let this happen.
You and me
In the heat of the moment.
But I'm never her.
I'm always watching it happen
Like I'm not even in the room,
But looking through a small hole
Dug into the wall.
I'm never facing towards you where I can see your face.
As hard as I try
I can never catch a glimpse.
Whenever you speak your voice is muted and it's all empty sound.
When I imagine the freedom of my release when the emotions begin
to flood
I always see me.
Falling, crying, weeping, screaming, shouting.
But I never see you.
You're there, but not really.
The bed between us seems so big,
It could cover the Atlantic Ocean.
And when it's over, you're gone.
My mind doesn't know what you look like during or immediately after
my catalyst
Because you're never there to see it.

Running Water

Tears for my mama really be tears for me.
A girl in the past who thought she'd never be.
Holding herself accountable for actions of another.
It sucks when you begin to understand the woes of your mother.
She told me to choose better, but how can I love?
I've learned there is no threshold for forgiveness above
This man's head as he screams he hates me and degrades me.
No greater hurt to see what I've become when I said that it ain't me.
I cry for my mama because she never knew love.
I cry for myself because I chose the same one.
Running water.
It's all running water.
Never ends.
I've become my mother's daughter.

Nigga Pay Me

Since you wanna act like you don't wanna
Claim me,
No need to wait six months and tell me that you're
Over it.
Bored.
Caught feelings for some other girl
Who's shows you the world
In her twirly and cute curls.
Since you wanna post up with your ex
And tell me there's nothing there.
It's nothing fair
That I was the one who initially curved you're bum ass.
But I took a chance.
Wanted a little sweet romance
With no games
And no feelings of insecurity.
Because I'm the Holy Saint called
Non Dairy
And all you want is my
Purity
How am I out yo broke down ass league
And still struggling into the last inning.
I never wanted to catch feelings.
But I did and now I'm waiting for you to act
Like you won the prize you so desperately chased.
But forget it.
I see myself in those others girls.

The ones you promised the world
But left broken and hung up on the hope.
That maybe he'll finally claim me.
Maybe he'll call me baby.
Maybe after six months
And late nights fucks,
Only to end up on the dump truck
And for you to move on so rapidly.
Nah, it's crazy how I see myself in those other girls.
Can't harp on a criminal for being
Framed for a crime
In which he did not commit
Because you always failed to commit.
What the fuck are commitment problems
But a man hiding behind a made up diagnosis,
Just to have his cake and eat it too.
But since you want to teehee and look at me
Saying, "Ooo imma play her."
Then let me tell you.
I'm not about to sit up
And act like your love strung baker.
Fuck you're cake, Nigga.
I didn't even buy the groceries
For your two teaspoons of good loving.
Great fucking,
Or the pound of unreciprocated loyalty.

You not gone foil me,
Professor num nuts.
Matter of fact, since we sitting at the dining table
With a feast of indecencies you've chosen to feed me
From the left over scraps handed down from
Tear drenched palms.
I'll cash out now and split the check.
How about you cover the gas I put in my tank
To drive miles and miles
To put on a pretty smile
And stroke your ego
While you freeload on my spiritual abundance.
Naw, Nigga, fucking pay me
For all my time wasted,
And then maybe
I'll leave out the ushy gooshy shit you don't want
Your boys
Knowing you said to me.
Actually, I'll disclose that for free.
Time to run your card for all my
Love
You did discard
And the sweatsuit of a person you made me dress up as
To be your fucking cheerleader from underneath the bleachers
And never seeing the light of your favor
With yo bitch ass.
Cover that

And I'll leave a tip
For the next woman you come across.
May her peace be kept
And her feet left unswept
From your lies and promises of a loving future.
May she see through you in ways I could not.
May she never experience the feeling of your embrace as I did.
Wishing to melt into it forever.
May she never feel how amazing and
Good
Your loving can be,
Only to know this form of you has been
Prerecorded
And made to order
For misfortunate women who got the same show
But never knew the venue stretched farther than these bedroom walls.
So that'll be my contribution
On this long running bill that I will be sending you.
And I want it in cash
Stacked tall like my ass
And green with envy for the woman
Who gets the finished product of a man I'll make you
to be.
I wished you'd never dated me.
Wished I never realized the truth in the things I see.
But I do now.
So Nigga, fucking pay me.

Not For Me

I guess I'm corny for wanting some romance.
I really wanted to slow dance with you
In your room,
Listening to the music my grandparents did.
The music my parents couldn't quite find the tempo to.
I'd lay my head on your chest and it would feel
Good.
I wanted to walk together on the street,
Lost in conversation.
For you to find something I said hilarious or
Intriguing.
For you to want to talk to me for hours,
But have every moment string together as if
They were all happening at the same time.
I really wanted all the dumb love stuff
People show in movies,
Or things people say they wish could happen.
I thought if I showed you how to love me,
Been the person I wanted you to be for me
And more,
I thought just maybe you'd think I was worth it.
But I guess that love isn't meant for me.
It's meant for someone else.
And I'm just standing in the way of someone else's great romance.

Wrong Address

You know,
I spent so much of my life dreaming about my
First love.
About how wonderful it would be.
How it would come out of nowhere.
Sweep me off my feet
And be like all the movies I told myself would
One day happen to me.
I wasn't stupid.
I always knew real life could be so much more
Boring
Than the movies.
But a part of me still believed it would have magic
Because what could be better than someone who
Loves you as much you love them?
Spend nights on pillows looking up at the ceiling
And wondering if both of you were thinking of
The other.
Going on sweet romantic dates and slowly falling for someone
Who you never thought in a million years could be real.
I knew it would be work.
I knew that there would be moments where things would be hard.
My dad used to tell me,
Mija, happiness is temporary
But joy is forever.
You have to find someone in life who you can
Build joy with.

Someone that when things get really hard
And you feel like giving up,
That little bit of joy you built together
Starts to warm the parts of your heart that've
Grown so cold towards one another
And allows you to begin again.
I would read up about love languages and
How to manifest the perfect person for myself
Even if their flaws masked their beauty
In their own eyes.
I learned from other's mistakes and told myself
When I got the chance,
I was gonna do it right.
I was going to show up to every accomplishment,
Listen and admit when I was wrong,
Make the other person feel heard and cared for.
Never make them feel like I didn't trust them to have
Friends of their own.
Be a partnership and not a codependency.
Give them space and allow them to grow as an
Individual,
And not just a part of something you find whole.
Give them gifts and small love letters.
Notes in their lunch about how proud they make you.
To love completely and without hesitation.
Out loud.
I thought to myself,
When I get a hand in love,
I'm going to do it right.

But I learned that
You can do it all.
Be the person you know the other needs,
Wants,
And desires.
Shower them with a boundless love
That exceeds all expectations set from the movies.
You can listen and hold on to their every word
And still not train your ears to hear what your
Heart denies to be true.
They could never want to ever love you.
Never crave the immense tenderness you make
Available to them,
And could whisper to you in inaudible volumes
That they never believed you were the one for them.
Just one of them.
A stop in their miles eye,
And nothing more but a glorious experience
That they'll pull from
To know how to treat the next one.
The one they deem worthy
And you will have been nothing more than
A lesson to them.
And as you sit there,
Cup running empty,
And trays of devotion devoured and gauged at,
You'll feel hollow inside.
You'll feel this heaviness on your chest,
And this betrayal to yourself of feeling like
This want,

This preparation for the perfect first love
Was squandered on months of feeling like
You can make it work.
You can fabricate the blueprint of magic
That if you just try harder.
Be more understanding
And wait it out.
Wait for the joy to kick in.
Then it'll somehow be worth it.
But you'll be waiting forever,
Because you can't fuel a fire with only one match lit
And the entire tin of gasoline poured on only one log.
You can't make someone see
What they believe is not there.
And so you'll learn the true meaning of unrequited love.
It isn't chasing after someone who doesn't even know your name.
It isn't just falling victim to a friend who wants to be nothing more
than that.
No,
Sometimes the worst form of unrequited love
Is looking at someone deep into their eyes,
Allowing your love to encompass them as they do desire.
To think they love you as much you love them.
For them to kiss you with passion at every
Break in breath.
To hold them close as you sleep.
And then for them to tell you one day
After it all,
It was never a relationship to them.
It wasn't enough,
And it never will be.

Buttered Tofu

The nature of love has changed.
½ cup of oat milk with ½ cup soaked cashew—blend together until silky
Smooth,
Like the ripple in my speech
When we speak.
I feel our melodies begin to peak like the moon.
A whole onion, four garlic cloves, medium piece of ginger, all
Minced.
Night sky twinkling further and further beyond twilight.
It was this night that I hoped you'd come through.
Make me believe that I had wrongly thought of you.
Betrayed the framework of your authenticity.
Say to me what I never thought was flesh.
Olive oil, medium heat. Sauté the minced vegetables until
Golden.
I find your aura enticing, but I'm no fool.
I know the origin of your rule against me.
Your puppeteer strings tied on my valves.
I recognize the hurt that I love so much because I
Masked it for passion.
No love without turn.

Oil the pan frequently. Season with coriander, chili powder, cinnamon, turmeric, onion powder, cumin, for the maple syrup. You must

Drizzle.

Give me what is left over of you.

The scraps you wouldn't dare give another man,

And I'll feast on it like a hyena deprived of its hunt.

Add in your cubed tofu and let the moisture steam out. Then add a can of tomatoes, butter, and your cashew

Cream.

Lathered up in dishonesty, expectance, poisonous self-doubt, as if it were nursing me back to health.

You fucking asshole.

Stir together.

It sat out all night.

I sat out all night.

Now look.

Both spoiled rotten.

Buttered tofu.

Playing Pretend

It's never felt like making love to me.
Inter looping my fingers with yours, I always
Turn away and wait for it to be over.
I hold you tight, begging to feel needed
Or desired.
Instead of what's there.
You don't even look at me.
Our eyes cross paths like strangers in the road.
Traveling down our own makeshift fantasies
We hope will do us in,
If only to satisfy some undying hunger.
A fear of loneliness even in intimacy.
Late at night, lights down, a slip over my knees.
A grandiose attempt to convince our audience that we're still in love,
Or ever were.
And in the morning when I wake,
I count the minutes until you make your escape.
Another day, another fill, and a bottomless void
Buried in my chest.
But maybe it'll fade for a moment
When you kiss me on my neck.
Stuck in bed,
Feeling like something that just hasn't realized it's already dead.

Dramaturgy

Now I'm sure I could write you a dozen love poems,
Capture the way distance becomes fictional beyond anything more than
physical to us.
I could go for hours discussing the ways I dream of you.
In the middle of the night when all the hours of business have passed,
And I'm left only with the residue that fuels the passion in my heart
to hear.
The low and rhythmic humming.
The persistent drumming of highs and lows,
And the warmth that fills my body
Until it glows.
I could write about us at the beach,
Eating small finger sandwiches that you undoubtedly cut way too small.
I could write about the way you kissed me that night by the lake,
And how I swooned by your urgency to break the distance between
our lips.
I could let my pen draw out pictures frame by frame
On how we traveled the world through the long talks on the phone.
I could discuss the way you showed me how to live again and to love
doing it.
Sure, I could write about the hard times, too.
How for nights I'd cry myself to bed so unsure of the future between us,
But also exploding with excitement that for once I had something I was
so terrified to lose.
I could write poems about those moments.
Walking away from the car and holding my arms close to my chest, if only
to save my still beating heart.
I could write about our make ups,
How they were often gentle and
Filled with hope and humility.
Where we both admitted how we were wrong,
And how we'd promise to be better for one another

How we believed each other to be true
I could write about our road trips that almost happened
Or the times where we felt our whole life was ahead of us and not
barreling down the turnpike like a high speed chase to nowhere
I suppose I could write about the song you wrote for me.
How I spent afternoons drinking in the sun,
Letting your aroma linger on the touch of my nose
And listened to the tune over and over again in my head.
There was no promise,
No guarantee of anything,
Just an escalation into tomorrow.
And another day
To write you another love poem,
Or I guess I could write about the moments you made me feel lonely
Where I wondered and fully believed that I had done something wrong,
Left me to sort through the mess you left me as
To build back up my piece of mind.
And then for you to come back when it was convenient for you
To make sure I never truly healed—
Damaged enough for you to slip back in,
But not too much to where I had nothing more to give
But an endless cycle
Of a new kind of renewable energy.
That you guaranteed an endless supply of
One I would never cut off.
You used to love the way I rambled,
The way I was honest and had passion for everything I grasped.
And then one day you looked at me like a bored child.
Maybe I'll write a poem about that,
And maybe I'll end it that way.
The way you once left me.
Unsatisfied.

Soul Sister Pt.2

Did you ever dream of our union,
Passed the point of being foolish with ourselves
And realizing we were anything but new to him.
Kindred hearts.
I have come to you now to say
I know
I know the depths of your pain,
The weight of its sting,
And all the things you wished to save me from.
That night upon meeting,
We stumbled to create a proper greeting
To one another.
I remember seeing you through that dirty glass window
Waving you over to let me in,
And seeing in your eyes,
In your hunch,
In the expression that held neither sadness nor content.
Just void.
When timelines did not merge but rather switched
And I had become part of the cycle of girls
Who believed this go round would be different.
How can I call to you in my time of need
That the future I saw in you was truly me.
Taking the same steps you once had
And becoming the intruder in a space once mine.
Is this a message from the divine?

Would it be too much to ask of your time
If I sent out for you?
If only for you to tell me this feeling gets better,
That my will power will not feather,
And I won't continue to accept indifference as a pacifier
For my aching wound.
Refreshed and renewed
At every glance for a second chance at love.
I now know the reason behind the embrace
That you flaunted in my face
To reveal his comfortability with unreciprocated devotion.
It was never about getting to him.
It was about showing me.
And it's something cruel that I cannot unsee.
I call to motion the ending of this pattern,
This unending cycle
Of broken love affairs having to be recycled
To every young woman who never learned wholesome love.
I only called to say thank you
For sitting where I would not stand
And unveiling to me the real man
Behind the one who I came to care for so deeply.
The end of this pattern has come,
And I've chosen not to repeat it.

It's My SHIT

My time.
Elongated and treated like a dime.
A quarter length and a fine
For the irreversible hymn and hum.
A drum up of all the fucking nights I sat up and waited for you.
Yo fuck ass postponing arrival until the sun fell beneath the tide pole of
boundaries I swore
I'd never let a man cross.
That's my mother fucking shit man.
My piece of mind that I was building up brick by brick
Until I built a sanctuary away from your bullshit
That spoiled the bed I promised to a future lover.
A home for the future mother I dreamed to be.
The one you claimed to see
Not so distantly in our timelines.
That's my fucking shit.
That's my slang, my ways.
The words that wrap around days
And simplify them into legends,
Myths,
And stories for fellow travelers on this earth.
You ain't fucking witty.
You don't even know the film titled Mitty,
About a middle aged crisis
That can happen to anyone.
Every deep thought.
Every daring glare.
Every confidently proclaimed sentence without a period.
That's my mother fucking shit.
That's MY shit.
And I want it back.

Denim Jeans

Uncertainty bellows beneath the cushions of my pillows at night,
Hiding underneath the bed frame like adolescent aged monsters.
I hate them and spend hours into the night wishing they'd go away.
They always seem to stay,
Claiming to be the me I wish to regift so that I'll fit next to your hip.
If I promised you more time,
It would only be to quiet what I know in myself to be true.
I don't know if I can only love you.
I can't say I'll feel this way for an eternity.
It seems so long to lay low with one
When inside I feel I must be free.
And my wings seem docile in your eyes that build brick by brick.
A future I wish I never cemented.
I think I'll slip away
At the store in the morning while you reach into your pocket.
The last image in my mind.
The torn out hole in your denim jeans.
I'm sorry,
But I can't stay.
I don't think these feelings of unquenched solitude will every fade away,
But stack beneath my pillows,
Where the monsters forever lay.

Door Swinging

And so
It ended.
I had said all the words I had come to know.
Sat much longer than I had ever intended
And listened to you break my heart one more time
As you told me you would never go more than halfway
Where I would give no less than exceeding what was required.
For the first time in months
I walked to my car alone,
Looked back to see if perhaps you'd chase me.
Realized you could never replace me
And tell me you were ready to love me
The right way.
But the air behind me grew colder,
A frigid feeling that had become foreign to me
And that night I grew a little older
And built strongholds around my heart,
So that I wouldn't feel this pain anymore.
I told you once I left
I wouldn't be walking back through that door.
I left it swinging.
No promises or room for a greater love
Anymore.

Surprised to See

You can prepare all you want
For what you know is not yet there.
Diminish every sharp pain that you feel
And convince yourself you don't care.
Begin a mindset that you believe will soften the blow.
You won't be disappointed in that person, that love
When their final dismal can't inform you of something you already know.
But the truth is that
You may see all the warning signs,
Travel the ends of the earth to make sure you'll be fine.
Guarantee no surprises when there's a snap from the final pull.
Make sure your embankment of self-love is completely
Full.
Think that when the day comes you'll know how to get through it and
won't let a tear fall.
But trust me when I say
There's no way to prepare for a heartbreak.
No way of preparation at all.

Farewell

Love has a funny way of leaving you.
When I was a kid I was never really fond of Mary Poppins—
A woman who one day just leaves,
And you never really have a chance to say goodbye.
But one day I woke up and realized we weren't fated for each other.
All those magical moments in the bathtub
Where we spoke about our coming together
And late nights where I swore it couldn't have been a coincidence.
I thought I was falling in love with you,
But just like the nanny in an old wives' tale,
One day my heart peered into yours
And decided it was time to leave

Part Three

LIFE

*(A deeper look within my family in both the aid
or harm in my own plight)*

*A reinspection of the root of our problems
and why they form, progressing into the person we finally become and
sadly mourn.*

Cast Away

Welcome home.
A banner without tack.
Wondering why I've come back.
Back to cookouts without a big enough attendance
To remember the family unity that never fully mended.
After years of broken solidarity hiding behind the
Veil of grief.
Promised myself the tracks left behind would never grow in depth from
back-tracking.
Reliving the past and hoping for a different outcome.
Missing the days I ran around with my shoes off,
Dirty footprints all over the kitchen floor,
And pushing my VHS tape in
Days watching old movies with my mom and my sister.
Newly trimmed hair after playing with the kitchen scissors.
Sprawled across the couch like a convening of self-leisure deans
And identifying with the femme fatale when she actually explains what
she truly means.
What she feels.
Going ashore to familiar doors that I pronounced stranger,
Like a young girl
Remembering to paint the colors in the wind.
Taking a cosmic spin back to the time when I was truly
Happy.
But now the room looks smaller.
Or perhaps I've just gotten taller.
But the way it makes me feel always stays the same.
Welcome home.

Saint

Come forward, brother.
Oh holiest art thou,
Whose sinking wounds have now
Proclaimed themselves healed.
Come forward my brother.
You've corrected your misdoings done upon man.
Women, all the women
Small and dainty and too young to realize—
Realize these walls would never leave them.
Those touches would remain permanent
That years later it did make a difference.
Oh, but forget all that my brother
Drinketh my cup as your own.
Grasp onto my hand as it is clean.
Dress in my same silk and call yourself
Saint.

A Saint amongst thickened thieves.
Playground giggles are now your doing.
No more battered little girls or sleepless nights.
No more sobbing late at night
That little girl's robe is tattered, dirty, and red.
But now you're clean my brother, so clean
A better you you've ever been.
Step forward and take your seat beside me
On this throne feathered with gold and crystal.
I care not of the packed bags and wishes of death
Of another.
I do not think of
The broken glass and cries of rescue.
No, that girl was simply a test, oh brother.
Her voice is too broken now to reach
The height of my ears,
So I keep them closed for you.
Oh brother,
For you are now a
Saint.

Playhouse Blues

I went to the playhouse with my dad and my sister.
It was at the Goodman theater.
The Christmas Carol.
The show that came this time every year.
My dad told me since he was a kid he had
Always dreamed of seeing it,
But never had the money,
But this year he got the tickets for discount.
The set was beautiful.
The transitions were artful,
And when the lights came up
I noticed we had been the only speck of brown in the crowd,
The only variation in hue that could be seen from my point of view.
How can we experience art
When it is kept from us
In Secret
And in prices.
With our wages,
I hate it here.
Keep your shows.
I'll make my own.

Stand by Me

I waited for hours.
The cookies all tore apart and turned rotten
By the door and the wind is still blowing.
My hat stayed perfectly still,
Like me.
Only me.
The disco lights twirled and danced
On the floor without skid marks
Or pools of sweat.
Every note of each song felt empty.
Take me by my string and boots.
I felt like I might see you.
See you or you.
Or even you.
I was there,
Standing tall and clapping
For feet walking across stages that weren't
Mine.
The wall claimed my name for
Countless events.
Events where I felt asked for but
Never needed,
Never treasured, nor loved all the way
The same pose for every picture.
Because pictures were never asked for.
The tolls of life will always take place
But I become Olympic to escalate my way to you,
For you, and
You and, even you.

Puppet Man

Can't you see I'm a
Puppet man.
A black and brown
Go and get 'em man.
Never taking what was never ours
Type of man.
Never involved but always watching
Type of man.
I'll never look away to what must be
Seen
By every eye and the eyes
I've seen.
You could never be a
Puppet man.
Throw away your every
Moral man.
Stand on broken legs
Type of man.
Tie me up and the noose is tight
Kind of man.
New accessory is riddled with hay water
Kinda man.
The blood of my sistas and brothers
Type of man.
But I hold your truth and know my lies.
I rebuke them.
I rebuke them,
I'm sorry, so I fight.

Never leave out of my sight but
My eyes are covered.
Taken hostage by my lover who I call
Home owner and tide cleaner.
The nearest storm has been centuries deep,
Fleeing coast to coast
But never leaves.
I love my newest noose,
I swear I'm tearing loose.
I pull and I heave my brotha.
Bring me your kin and loving motha'.
I'll protest thee but hold dear to my heart.
My gun is tethered to my art.
I swear I was just trying
To play my part.
But I never knew my truest home
Was broken down
And was never fully known.
I shut my mouth and quiet your screams.
You have a face,
 a skin like me.
But I will forever simply be
A model in burning sand.
Wounds growing deeper and more
Grand.
Oh sweet sista and suffering brotha,
I am but
A puppet man.

Papa a Mi Papa

No day passes without the small smile I was blessed to see.
The cold eyes that grew warm for me.
Love of a father that wasn't mine
The silent type without gifts or a loving embrace.
Bowls of mole with sweet chicken that
You cooked.
I can't even remember your name.
Como mi espanol
Mas bien que todos anos despues de mi tiempo con usted
Di me come come come mija
Tranquilla porque yo tengo tu tarea
You taught me that silence could be loving and a home when darkness
seemed so much more
Comfortable.
You were my dad when I thought I didn't have one.
Porque usted es el papa a mi papa
El abuelo siempre quiero y
Lo siento Enrique
Lo siento
Yo quiero usted
Necessito gracar a usted
Para todo
Porque tu comida estaba mas que comida
Esta mi casa pero una casa en el corazón
Mercido mas
Ahora...mercienda mas
Siempre
Gracias Enrique
Gracias
Y necessica que saber
Te extrano
Extrano mucho

Gingerbread Home

Press your ear against the walls
That were once paper thin.
Plastered to a thickness suitable enough
To build a home—
A home for us three.
Battered and uneasy,
Laying our heads on claimed soil.
In times of toil, I wonder if maybe
Our hearts will give out for the last time.
We'll grow rotten and shun each other
From the world that never showed us kindness
Or forgiveness
For the misdeeds they committed against us.
Why do our mouths open wide to laugh
Rather than cry when the rubber on the tire
Folds in on itself
And bursts all over the asphalt?
When the world around us crumbles,
Why do we ride the slippery slope
Down, down, down?
To enjoy the ride and know that we experienced it,
That we survived it,
And that it's too funny to know that we
Have become the center of a dark comedy.
Twinkling lights from years past that fade and fade
In our eyes that remained glazed with hope,
Through the emerging window in the evergreen blades.
To feel merry at this time and take our joy
In each other's presence
With empty pockets
And a tree without many presents,
But the biggest gift which were the keys to doors.
We signed our names
On the brink of tears, but smiling because at least I have you when all the
dust clears.

Chinese Take Out

On this chilly Christmas Eve,
Without a hoo or a shout.
Not a creature was stirring
Not even a mouse.
Me and my mom's had stopped to grab some Chinese take out
Because we didn't have a single pot or pan in the house.
All the cupboards were bare without a whisper or a hare.
No plentiful fridge.
No grand Christmas Eve feast.
No big glazed chicken fresh out the oven.
Just a mom and her two daughters splitting a meal meant for one,
And my sister shoved the food meant for us two
In her mouth to chew.
I rose in anger from my chair against the wall,
Screaming about how that food wasn't completely hers,
Not even at all.
So we all screamed at each other and at Mariah who cried
For a joke that went too far and a sadly spoiled appetite.
But we weren't mad at Mariah for putting her fingers and mouth all over
the food.
I wasn't mad at my mom for always blaming me for things I did not do.
But because it was Christmas Eve and we were fighting with great fines
Over a small plate of Vegetable lo mein that was $9.49.

Cadillac Karma

We've sat and wondered.
Told ourselves, "Something's gotta give."
Because if things kept as they were
Without question we would surely die.
We thought
God chose us to fight these heavy battles,
Allowed suffering before our final blessing,
And let our anchored tears turn into quickened heart beats
From laughter that would never cease.
You always told me this type of life required humor
And I believed you because imagine if we couldn't
Laugh every time the car broke down,
Chuckled when the heat was turned off,
Reeled back in our chairs when every person in power
Denied, declined, and refused to revive
The hope in our eyes that dwindled with every steel shut door.
Or the shouting that just wouldn't stop.
Days that cracked like egg shells beneath our feet
But we told ourselves our eyes hadn't grown
Heavy with anguish,
But collected interest that God would one day cash in.
Things are always so hard before something really big happens,
Right?
So I guess ten years must mean the biggest break
Of our lives.
Just stick around a little while longer, mom
I promise I'll make things right.

Please Breathe

Can I please just catch a break.
Worrying about my car and its brakes,
And this month's rent I might not make.
And wondering if his feelings have always been fake.
And I'm trying not to hesitate when it comes to
Talking about how I feel.
Am I healed?
Are all those things people say in spiritual twitter even real?
About manifesting and believing,
And how you're never truly done healing,
And these bouts of sadness and anger
Have a deeper meaning that I must wager
Against myself and my ego.
But why do I feel like I'm becoming an emotional freeloader.
Countless texts, like am I alright?
The millionth hour in this internal fight.
With taking a break but feeling like I didn't earn it.
Please.
Can I have a moment to just breathe?
Can the hardship take a back seat
And wait till I turn a corner into prosperity and soft melodies
In my happy ending or come up that I'm just waiting for,
The one I'm praying for?
Just one day.
One day.
Where things can be warm.
Things can be whole.
Things can be easy.
I just need one day.
One thing
To go right.
Is that alright?

Self-Council

Too many times I wonder what things you would have said.
Would you like the man he is,
The man he promised to become?
Or would you recognize identical tears in my eyes
Twenty years apart from my mother?
Sit me down on your porch and tell me,
"He's not for you, baby."
And would I listen.
When he cancelled the other night
And I told myself it was normal
To be understanding and know that I can't be his
First priority.
But then I heard you say,
"Baby you can't keep thinking that way
If a man wants to see you, he'll see you.
Is any man worth the amount of tears you've shed?
Or the nights you've stayed up
If only to get the scraps of his time."
And I cried knowing those words have been said before
To a young woman whose womb had bore
The same timeline in me,
In hopes of a different outcome.
But I can't help but feel torn the same way she did
In the way my heart feels defeated,
Not knowing how to navigate trauma or projection
Or know if my sense of love is going in the right direction.
And I feel robbed that you were taken so soon.
I wish you could tell me what to do,
Or if I could muster up more words than the same few.
Because Grandma I really miss you.

A Loss for Words

I think my mistake was that I sought for you
In peoples embraces and their
Blank faces that I hoped would warm for me
The way yours always did.
I'm standing on the platform looking around every beam
I'm hoping the final stop won't be passed our meeting.
To remember what it was like riding around with you
In the white van before it gave out,
When you'd make me sit in the back until I convinced you I'd be safe
upfront with you.
Pulling into the drive thru at McDonalds and buying me
One too many double cheeseburgers and pies,
Because there were too many times you went to bed
With an empty stomach at the end of the night.
And every performance I forgot to tell you about,
But you somehow showed up for.
Times as a kid where I never knew how to want more
Or need it.
I'm standing on the platform where my shoes no longer have Dora
on them.
Where my lunchbox isn't colorful,
And my time isn't mine anymore.
I looked around every beam
And I can't see you.

Return to Sender

You bitch nigga.
I apologize for my profanity,
But lately you've been playing with my sanity.
Gaslighting with a blow torch.
Light me up and burn it down.
Like yo babies who was on the porch.
I'm twice the man you'll ever be.
And what's funny is that we don't have the same anatomy.
What's even funnier is that you always doubted me
To be the one stepping up for the family.
While you chased out and ran
From your responsibilities as a man
And I had to become
A husband, a father, a mother.
Over the years and in a day
While my mother cried to my brother
About how she didn't know what to say
About the countless let downs and jobs you couldn't keep,
But your bed was where you would sleep
While my mama was on the couch trying to silence her tears
Under the thin veil of anger that she wore as the.
Strong black woman shield that so many wear.
I'm more of a man, more of a husband,
More of a decent human being than you'll ever be.
Putting groceries on the table without a receipt saying
"Owed to me,
Gratitude, benevolence,
And respect I never earned.
It was bought, and offers no returns.
Now take these burns and keep the ashes
In that ern
That I'll stop on."

Man, straight pathetic.
Waking up at the break of dawn to take my mama to work
While you laid up talking about how you heard they hiring
Paramedics,
But you didn't fill out the paperwork.
Didn't sign up for classes,
Just a whole bunch of more bullshit
While you continue to show your ass and
It's tiring.
That's right, McDonald's is hiring,
And if you don't take your sorry ass up there and let go
Of your pride,
How can you even look me in the eye?
When you know you've taken so much from me.
Taken childhoods—
My sisters and mine.
The reason why 911 is always on the line,
And new zip codes start to feel familiar when the patterns
Stay the same.
The start of me realizing most men are to blame
For either being bystanders like my father,
Enablers like your sons,
Or the coward that done it.
I pay bills
Unlike you.
Thought my mom would struggle without you.
Realize you were right.
Put me out on the street.
My maker
Is who you thought I'd meet
By the end of my first week.
But I'm not weak.

Do you know who the fuck I am?
Do you know whose name I claim?
All the woman you claimed would never be the same
After you trenched through their lives like a monster?
You broke me
When I thought I was unbreakable.
Made me feel small
When I spent so many years in counseling trying to feel
Big again,
And on Christmas break when I came back from school,
You made me feel fourteen again.
Made me realize I wasn't all healed and good now,
Like things were too distant from me to affect me now
But over the counter Band-Aids can't cover up the major wounds to my
soul that you caused.
For so long I wished that you'd get what was coming to you.
But now when I look at you,
A broken man,
Doors once opened to you now bolted shut,
I can't help but feel sorry for you.
You had the chance to be blessed.
Inducted into a family that allowed you to never address
Your past that was riddled with wrongdoings and red flags.
And now I see you limping,
Begging for another chance.
Because you realized we were never the burden of your life,
But the one thing keeping it going.
Your sorrys don't even work anymore.
Your promises all sound the same.
And now I see myself
A young woman
Who had to become a man.

Blue

Sometimes I wished you knew what I meant.
The pain that I feel deep inside being tucked away for
So long,
That when I get even a shiver of the feeling I know is there
I feel like a little kid again.
You're right.
You make more sacrifices than me.
You have more weight on your shoulders
But you hold me to your standard and
Forget that I'm supposed to be
Young.
Waking up and feeling trapped in these paper thin walls
That couldn't bar me from the profanities
Tied to my name
On the porch of decades of trauma that you built for
Me to rest on.
Begging but never receiving the chance to even drive
Five miles around the block
To clear my mind.
He screamed into me the things I'd never do.
And so I walked,
And I worked
Until I saved up every penny to buy my car.
My freedom.
My momentary escape.
My chance to build a life of my own,
But here now I still drive for you.
Bend to your schedule,
Because now you're without a car
And I'm forced to forget the times I was without one
And you let your husband deny me access.

Safe Shoulders

Days turned into years.
Hours never melted without a crease
And I forgot how you felt.
I used to run to you with both arms stretched.
My smile not ceasing even when you tossed me in the air.
I never became scared or doubted your willingness
To catch me.
Eighty degree weather with the sun beating on my neck.
You'd pull me over your shoulder
And carry me back to the car when long walks in the
Flea market
Tired me out.
You were my first love because you weren't my father,
But a man I trusted and held onto at family gatherings,
Hiding behind your legs when people spoke.
But I couldn't understand
The energies that rose in their throats and ejected onto your ears.
I found my hands learned to reach for you as if
The latter was unnatural.
Held onto your hand as you lead me into her room.
Coloring books still on the table.
Your shoulders had become my home,
Until they hovered over me so.
Then days turned into years
And I hadn't recalled until
Senior year Psychology
Where my teacher discussed how we
Dealt with trauma with fear.

An Interview with the Divine

Can I just ask why?
If given the time,
To know why my life was chosen.
To endure this unending suffering
Allowed by the Holiest Divine.
Have I taken too many rays of sunshine
From someone else in a far off or previous lifetime?
One I cannot recall,
But at some point knew was once mine.
Would it be brass of me, oh highest of all creators,
To ask for a moment where things of misfortune
Could come a little later?
I just know you must have a blessing for me.
One that mounts and gives validity to all the things
That happened, not periodically, but all at once
And crushed me when I thought I already stood
before you a broken women.
Would I be wrong to ask for an answer
To help me understand why all this hurt really matters
In crafting me to be the one you deem worthy
Of plentiful feasts without an empty cup
And unbreakable stature?

I ask only now,
What lesson am I supposed to obtain
In order to praise you? I must refrain
From questioning every tear in my polyester.
My heartache cannot continue to fester
Into resentment and hate for the world
When as a girl I wished only to be a naive jester
To dance and frolic through
This enlightening journey I joined with you
And promised to let you guide,
While I feathered my ensuing eyes
Closed.
Oh please Lord, know I trust you
And I'll keep on, no matter my plight.
But please, I beg of you God,
Help to make things go back right.

Southern Hospitality

I wanna sit on the wooden steps,
Droplets running down your glass as you drink lemonade.
Wanna hear the glass clink as you drink it down
One gulp at a time
And sway my feet by the riverbend before
The sun empties your tall glass.
I want your smile to touch my ears and soothe my fears.
For tomorrow
Your kindred spirit does not possess energy for me to borrow.
But rather, a seed that I desire,
But one you already once planted in the seedling before me.
Look out at the blades of grass
And hear the music the wind chimes create between each blow.
You'll struggle to your feet when the timer dings.
I'll jump without any barrier
And there,
Two women of the same fruit
At different ends of time.

Mama de Mi Papa

I'm sorry
If I disappointed you with the same heartbreak they've given to you.
Watching your feet continue to grow underneath the socks that are
supposed to help the pain go away.
I miss you terribly,
But I'm afraid you'll think that's a lie.
Everything I do is for you.
I hope to give you the glory they robbed of your time.
The promises they made but never fulfilled
You are the strength
That people think I have,
But never knew it was simply an impersonation
Of the woman you've always been.

Winkie

It'll be small things,
Like the soft touch of someone else's palm,
Or the warm glow in someone else's eyes,
Or a switch in someone's voice when they're speaking to me.
I was at work.
The women were old, but they pushed each other and fell back into youth
like it had become second nature to them.
Celebrating another year as if the clock of time wasn't ticking
against them.
You should be here,
With your cigarette tucked behind your ear,
Your deep burgundy lip liner and cheetah print Shaw.
The walker that had become an extension rather than
A restriction.
Journeys to the cupboard where you hid snacks behind the soup cans.
I learned about the woman you were after you died,
And I wonder what you would have said about the woman I've become.
My lips will barely part if only to let my soul speak what my flesh will
not allow.
To have divine intervention and feel your fragile hugs after dialysis.
I'll see you in the wrinkle of their eyes and smiles when they say I look
like a granddaughter of theirs.
Of all the deaths I could suffer,
None could come close to that I will endure when my mom dies.
I am almost twenty,
But I feel like I'm eight again walking around the pool with my floaty
searching for my mom to dive in with me.
I fear I'll drown without her if I'm already struggling to stay afloat
without you.
At your funeral, I pushed my tears to the surface,
To pay my debt I felt I owed to you,
Only to realize the sorrow would only multiply when I became a woman I
wish you knew.
The one who grew into the strength you passed down the grapevine.

Family BBQ

Before they died,
It was nothing but constant light.
Every few nights I'd be sharing the floor with
Kids with neighboring names and bloodlines
That crossed one another.
Full house with everyone pouring through the door
And more.
We'd all gathered in the basement and play
While our parents talked the night away,
And oldies brought them back to their youth they thought they still had
time to enjoy.
And once Winkie left,
So did their heart
Because they knew every look at each other's face
Would only remind them of what was missing,
And that common warmth they knew was more than a feeling,
But a promised unity they thought could never fade
Until it did.

Crossword Puzzles

Mimi collected word searches like they were going out of style.
Dragging her highlighter through each page
And never throwing them out right away
But stacking them
High like the Eiffel Tower all over the room.
She handed me one as she walked over to her favorite seat on the couch.
She slouched
And her eyes became heavy with exhaustion.
I held your hand as we walked quietly into the next room.
The bed was comfy
Until it wasn't.
I liked wearing those shorts
Until I didn't.
I loved our games
Until I didn't.
The leaves outside changed too many times to count,
And all I can remember is the
Stack of word search books
Hazy under the lamp light.

You Never Said Sorry

There are so many times I'll think about how much I love you.
How much losing you will hurt.
How my heart will simply leave when you do.
I'll spend my days wondering how to fill the emptiness,
But on our worst days I remember
We weren't always one.
Tears fell down my cheeks.
I told you I didn't recognize you behind your
Youthful mask.
That you were changing because of him.
You scared me
So much that I wanted it to end—
All of it to end.
Because I knew all that would come in the future
Would only make me hate you
And I didn't want to hate you.
I told people that I knew wouldn't care enough to
Call you.
And when you took away my phone
I thought you'd cry.
Ask me why I would do it.

If the door had slammed any harder,
It would have broken.
If you had moved any faster
I wouldn't have seen the look on your face as you
Smacked me.
A tingle sensation on loop.
You wanna be crazy?
You wanna be in the hospital?
I just wanted you to see me.
Wanted you to see that I was suffering
And that you were the one person I thought would
Protect me.
But how could you know to love my pain
When it was the same pain that took your mother
From you
In the middle of the night?
When she was dragged,
Never carried
To a place where she didn't belong.
I'm still hurting
And you never said sorry.

Stella

Oh Stella my girl,
How could I ever forget to mention you.
Cast you out.
Ruin your heart with abandonment.
You saw so many moments in my life
And held onto them
When all I wanted was to let go.
Cradled me in your arms
When I had nowhere to go.
Saw beach days and sandy feet
Where my nephews learned to understand joy,
And how to never let it go.
Late nights with friends talking about
How small the world can seem
When it doesn't stretch beyond your gaze.
Recklessly driving and praying to God.
Please don't let the police pull me over.
Hard times.
When my heart became too broken to fix overnight
And when rainy nights stretched into days.
You were there when the college boxes
Turned into garden boxes
And room for groceries in my backseat.
When growth was more than reuniting with old friends to go to the
drive-in.
You were there when I found me again.
When I fell in love with the person I was meant to be
And always was.
When I stretched my hand up to the sun
And forgot about doubt in this life.
When I realized human connection is one of
The most precious things in this life.

You saw trays of thanksgiving food and
The big Christmas tree we finally got.
You saw women become independent and love each other.
Long drives to see some stupid boy,
And sneaking out to parties,
Or seeing the same smiling girl.
Me coming out of that stupid boys house for the millionth time.
You were the one who became my other half.
My home away from home
And my safe passage.
And every time someone told me
Get a new one, this one's dingy,
I'd say of course not.
Because you were my girl.
When you started to fall apart
I kept saying this couldn't be your end.
It felt like we had so many more lifetimes to live together.
But as I watched you
A limp turning into an ongoing issue
And problems becoming worse,
I knew our time together would come to an end,
And so I bought a new one.
She's not you,
But that's okay.
You need to recover.
And when you do,
We're going back to the beach to see more sand.
I'm taking you to the drive in and getting extra popcorn
And we'll drive back downtown to see that stupid boy.
And you'll always be my girl.

When There's No One There to Listen

I think the walls hold the air that
Won't stick.
My ears are bleeding.
The eardrum torn from the words you've said.
But my mouth ran dry from things
I could never say.
My fingers flicker towards a screen,
Searching for untainted minds that
Don't know my name.
There's a hurt inside that I can't explain.
From the unwanted touch
The glances that linger for
Too long.
Those shorts too tight.
You're growing into a woman.
A woman I am,
But to you I'm not that
Type of woman.
I'm a young woman,
Not a sexy one.
Happy Father's Day.
A father of a father,
So slick your tongue slithers.
The devil, but the Adam for
Misguided Eve.
A Virgin Mary with sunken eyes and
A bloodied womb never healed.
I see the trauma in your eyes and I hoped
It wasn't transferable,
Consumable,
Eating away till it's made its home
In my burrow.

Rape, what if I raped her?
Touch.
What if I touched her?
Protect me, pick me up,
Carry me on your shoulders with my legs.
Spread.
My legs are spread
They're wide open,
They're spread.
Smiling, giggling,
Are you still tickling me?
The panty line promiscuous.
The brown girl traveler waving from
My legs.
Eyes wide in trust and not realizing
What was happening.
It's our favorite game.
Pull it tighter, tighter.
Pull them up more.
Wanna play again?
Let me smell, I really love the smell.
Do you trust me?
What if she said I raped her?
She's a liar.
If I were your age,
You're the finest one.
Movie maker.
Hopeless romantic.
Eyes glued to the tv.
Watch the love you want to see.
The love you wish you learned.
The love you wish you knew.

You're not scared, baby.
You're torn to shreds, and the pieces have been burned.
The ashes are scattered in the bullfight
Of the winds.
Blowing.
They're already gone.
You like the sounds that you hear between the thin walls.
I can make them happen for you, too.
Come here.
Do you even remember?
Everything feels so hazy.
The countless hands tied to blood—
Blood spilt from the same veins.
You can't remember anymore
The pathways have been severed.
Connecting could be fatal.
Remember.
You can remember.
You're body already has.
But it's lying.
You're a liar.
You've always been a liar.

Current Location

Where were you all when I needed you most?
Where were you, Dad, when you started to boast
About being a better father but claiming I'm doing the most?
For begging you to take us out of hell's fire before Mariah's
innocence broke.
Don't come to me now and ask for forgiveness.
When actions don't meet words that you're solely benefiting.
Sitting at night relishing in your pride,
But did you ever stop to proclaim remorse in my eyes?
Did you stop to call me and say I was worth the fight
When the tyrannical devil caused chaos throughout the night?
When we slept in cars and on mattresses
That never were ours.
Did you ever seek justice beyond the affirmations in your car?
Where is the action that is not temporary,
When we stop tolerating abuse because he's the man that we married.
Did I ever hesitate when I was young and without love
To show you the lengths I'll go from above?
I sat with my bags and thought about running,
But even my sister grew to think truest freedom is too stunning.
To have your voice carried without sin,
To know my story and know where I've been.
When am I an adult and not a child worth ignoring.
When I wake up in the night begging for the tears to stop pouring.
Was I wise for my age to constantly want levity,
Or was my youth simply robbed from all the adults who wouldn't keep
my life steady?
I had friends my own age who held me as I cried,
As we collectively promised it would never happen in our own lives.
When we were older and with kids
The same as we were,
Where were you all when my age became a blur?

Pillow Talk

A deep wrenching in the chest.
Grease the pulpit of your humility.
Leak into their pores like an IV,
Pushing what you consider essential to their bodies
As they dissipate and rot in the inside from
Metabolic fluids.
The hairs begin to stand.
Skin raises into curvatures and flaws.
Only closed eyes can see
Gnawing until drawing blood.
Piercing sounds like the days of old.
An emptiness
Never filled.
Abyss.

The Beauty In Silence

Mi abuelita.
Holding herself in her chair with what strength she has left.
Feet pressed against the same floors that have gone unswept.
Looking to the window in a stare unknown to me,
Not in discontent or heartache but in peace for what the world may be
As it's beaten her, robbed her, stolen much joy.
In these moments we relish in each other's silence I realize absence of
words is not something to avoid.
We both sit and smile but hers slowly fades
As she sits by her windowsill
Counting down her days.

The Essence of Time

When is the time for black women?
When is the time for Black Death
To no longer sit under floorboards swept
Paying the white man in debt
Of tears and internal fears we've wept?
When is the time for black women?
No clock for the sock you find in black women.
Not the idealization who you recognize as black women
But the darker the pigment for black women.
When is the time for black women
To no longer begged to be saved from black men?
To stop asking us to fall without mutual respect
Without warrant for life and not only value in death.
When is the time for black women?
Is it when you fall in love with us
Or when you find the comparison in lust
To say it's only the light skins you trust.
Only protecting your fetishes without a fuss
While our bodies pile up in the dust.
When is the time for black men
To step up and assert their desire to defend

All the frontline solitudes within the pen
They've helped create towards dark skin?
Calling us dark and dirty without feel of sin.
When is the time for black men
To stop calling on us when the world is fin,
And they expect us to fill up with streets but won't lend
Their solidarity against our metal tin.
You put us in but do not identify
Black women in the form of trans lives,
And think there's a difference between the value in eyes.
Stop thinking there's truth in your lies,
Because we're fighting for the liberation of black lives,
Not so you can come home to your ideal house wife
And switch spots with our common oppressor
While dressing in the same clothes in his dresser.
It's these thoughts in my mind I can't render,
And that's why we argue about being your true defender.
When is the time for black women?
When is it the time for black women?
When is black women?

Winkie's Wisdom

My grandmama had a lot of wishes,
I don't exactly know all the real specifics.
But I knew that she believed in family and keeping us together.
Even when our patience has grown the thinnest
When people tell me what I'm not,
I think about the women who showed me what I am,
I grew up in a home of strong women.
My great grandma, Mi abuelita, my grandma Winkie, and my mother.
Who loved me unconditionally and showered me with wisdom and truth.
I was convinced my grandmama winkie was a woman of wonder.
She used to pull out her fur coats at the dark of night.
Paint on her makeup like an artist at work,
The curving of her thin wrist- slipping and dropping the pencil on
the floor.
But a lady never wastes her time on picking up things of no worth,
That's what she would tell me.
Her cheetah print blouse and her high heels,
All to be shown from the limit of a wheelchair.
My grandma and papa would go to the boats like they were millionaires
on top of the world, only to come back in the morning and realize.
Her fragile bones would break from the sound of a whisper,
Her years on dialysis had people thinking that God had missed her,
I'd ask her how she did it, acting so strong for people who knew
her weaknesses
She used to say you always go out looking your best, cuz honey you never
know who you might see.
I thought how can a woman look so strong and be so weak,
And then I grew up.

My Own

I had a lover,
Rested in my quickened breath,
Called slumber in my nights.
It's a solo venture into my plight.
Why does peace erase me in this fight.

The Frosty Musketeer

Deep within the Tundra mountains,
Laid a frosty musketeer.
He indulged in reckless life,
In which was bereft with many fears.
Coated in blankets of snow,
Sat the poor miser.
Who now wished he traveled where climates are much higher.
He laid there seemingly dead,
But all that watched knew better
The Frosty Musketeer could never die,
His power to change into anything he touched,
Kept him light as a feather.
And unto tragedy the Musketeer makes do
He sprung up from his seat and screamed aloud, "Boo."
But no one was there,
In this small cave in the mountains.
All had died but years early on,
Before the avalanche struck the town.
Which gave the frosty musketeer his powers,
But killed his family,
And all those around
So to this the musketeer said, "Alas, it's too early in the day, I shall take
another 100 year nap and will hope to see my family in May."
Why because May was when the snow had already melted
And the snow came out to play.
But the Musketeer would never see his family again,
No matter the amount of days.
So to the musketeer we say, "Good luck."
And send him on his way.
Because no matter the amount of powers
A troubled heart will always remain.

Raggedy Old Man

And now I come to you
Within my pew
In sanctuary that I have offered to you.
Yet you remain cold.
Claim wisdom because you've grown old
But fail to meet the passion tensions.
And here in this I cannot forget to mention
That it is not simply with a bat of an eye
Or the single twitch between you and I.
Have I found in this I have truly realized.
Age does not solely bring wisdom.
Though you shrink back at me even now,
And take on this role of the book of the town,
I remind you of your place.
For your inner child and innocence was never meant to fade.
Never meant to look in daze and confusion.
The truest evil hidden within your stacked provisions
Against me.
But I offer the truth in the words now of the youth
That you were meant to hear now in me.
And see the call to act so vividly
In your mind,
In the way you remember it in your eyes,
In the way that I remember it in mine.
When you marched for civil rights to sit
Only to claim the same chairs when youth blood filled the air.
And you looked down at them with their brains filled with noise
As their wisdom grew and you quieted their voice,
Down your nose bridge with your armored texts.
On past times you still would like to remiss
About saying the only thing black youth favor
Is the incessant drive within our labor
From money.
Is it money you think I seek to hold.

A choke over in my new found mold.
Oh my honestly grows in you as you feel yourself
Beside me in your pew and I wonder
Has it all just been thunder?
Have the clamor of your youth slipped away
When you hoped to question every new day
And stopped fearing the world around you as it changed
Instead of over talking.
Listened so that I'd stayed
But I left you in your rotten pew
Because there was no need in talking to you
In a structure of word you clearly created
And abiding by it you hesitated.
Because education was not what you seek,
But a simple matter we could have done in a week.
But as you fail to list the news sources beyond a filter
That unfortunately does not include Twitter.
When just like birds a message can carry
Over oceans across to traumatize the wary.
And now you stand before me
Not knowing the current state of history
And letting your youth slip between the noise.
All the ways you've paid into the toys
That strangle them in their breath.
So when youth comes to you
With more than what you claim to be news,
Do not be surprised if we stand in disillusion of the two
Of when the same people who claimed walked in the civil rights
Can't seem to recall the way the media depicted
Their fight.
But it's alright,
For the youth will not be silenced,
Or old within their ignorance.
It is you who will lack what the true word is
And do to you a greater disservice.

The Blue Winged Angel
Will Fly Away at Once.

Oh Blue winged Angel, you took away my pain and taught me how
to smile.
You hid away your emptiness and road ahead for half a mile.
I buried you inside my heart the day you began to leave,
I didn't want to believe you were truly gone,
I didn't think it was my reality.
It takes years and years to truly cherish something lost long ago,
Oh blue winged angel I wish you'd take me away from this life that
I inhabit.
Grandma I didn't love you enough when you were here with me,
Guiding my hand across the cupboard doors,
I took advantage of our time and saw you as an automatic rather than
a privilege,
When times are hard, even now, I call your name into the night sky.
Blue winged Angel your feathers are crisp to the touch,
I take in your warm touch against mine and take solace in your company.
Blue winged Angel please come back, I plead, even if it's only for
the night.
When everyone has already fallen asleep, and the floor is creaky at
the touch.
Blue winged Angel please come back, you're the only one I trust.
Grandma I should have hugged you one more time.
I should have told you how much I needed you.
Instead of asking who you are, I should have asked you who you were.
I promise I cared, I promise I loved you.
You were my tiger lily.
I wish I hadn't wasted so much time with my very own blue winged angel.

Part Four:

GROWTH

*(The ability to nourish your own soul
and fuel the seeds of Love)*

*An ability to realize the right or wrong in the way you feel
and being given the chance to cut down certain trees and begin to replant
your own seeds.*

A Year Alone

(Written For My Speech Class the Fall of 2019)

Birthdays. There's a big cake and decorations and all these people around celebrating you. One day in the entire year where the attention and the time to be made feel special is for you. But how special can you feel if the party's attendance is only one?

When I graduated high school I decided to attend DePaul University for film because it seemed safer than theater. When I went I was so excited to meet new friends. During previews at DePaul, they decided to have a barbecue where freshmen could hang out and get to know each other. That's where I meet them—Sela, Sadie, and Ahmari. From the moment I met them it felt like all the years of previous false friendships had finally led up to these real ones.

Sela, Sadie, Ahmari and I were immediate best friends. We'd feel so grown up going over each other's dorms and talking until 4 AM. One of us would get sick and we'd all go to the store and get chicken soup and Tums and the little soft tissues for each other with the last twenty dollars we had to our names. We'd sit right next to each other laughing and yelling at each other and not care about the possibility of all of us getting sick—because even if we did all manage to infect each other, then at least we'd be able to stay home—sniffling and coughing all over each other. But being together.

There were moments, one moment during the Thanksgiving dinner we had cooked with one another and I felt like I was looking around at the future aunts and old women—bickering about if aliens were real or if mermaids were really at the bottom of the ocean. Laying there singing songs acapella off key and feeling like these were the women I was going to start my life with.

I'm towards the end of my freshman year in college and I have a job that works me forty-five hours a week as a busser in a five star restaurant until 3AM. My dad had told me I needed a job and how if I somehow didn't work myself to the ground because that's what us Mexicans do then I was somehow not earning my degree like he had done. And I've been super busy working and taking care of the people back home. My best friends at home—Jill, Cristian, Carmen and I stop talking after a few conversations about me not being enough.

So I'm my way home to my dorm from work and I'm calling Sadie and Sela and Ahmari to see if I can come over to talk about everything. And then I find out they'd been talking about me behind my back, and hanging out without me. And Sadie tells me they didn't want to be friends with someone who didn't have time for them anymore. That we were adults now. And I'm standing there in the cold, shivering, and crying like a mess. And there's aching pain in my chest that I can't quite explain to you. It's like you're empty and the people you once loved stole any Heart you had left to even be able to understand why you're crying or how long the tears have been falling. And you just feel alone.

This is the moment in the story when I tell you even though I came home and cried alone all night when I've been there to hold others. That even though I stayed up long nights because someone needed an ear to listen but couldn't get a single person to answer at eleven. That while I had given up so much of me for those I loved—this is the moment where I'm supposed to say this was the worst. But you'll have to wait for that.

I decided to come home. I enrolled at Prairie State College, and decided that I'd be alright. Life has a funny way of making you feel what it wants you to feel. When you try to run away from the lessons life has in store for you, it has a way of making you face it one way or another.

One day at work, we had a party of old black women sitting around a table and they get up—all except one—and start to sing. They start singing Happy Birthday. They're clapping and singing and having such joy in their hearts for this one person. But when I looked into the joy of the birthday woman's eyes—I did not see my own. And I don't know why, but I started to think about my birthday and how it was coming up. And how last year there were only two people there. And I thought after the Sadie, Sela, Ahmari situation—after the Jill and Carmen situation—after Cristian, after it all that, THAT was when I felt the most alone. But I was wrong.

It was this moment right here feeling like I was seeing something that I may never one day have- this is when I felt my most alone. I wanted to tell someone—anyone—but who could I tell? Really? Moments when everyone leaves you without any real reason why starts to make you think the only thing wrong is you. That you somehow deserve all the heartbreak and hurt inside. So here's my warning- this was the worst.

I spent a long time after that. Completely off social media. I disappeared in a sense, and started working on me. The first days were hard, but this is the part where I tell you things got better. All that time alone starts to make you see who you are when no one's around. I found out I'm actually a really good cook. That I'm actually really smart, and I mean Ivy League smart. I found out I'm more quiet than I thought I was. And that I like dark chocolate in my banana pancakes. And I also realized I'm an amazing friend, and kind person- and someone who was never truly the problem.

They say you don't appreciate something until it's gone. And one day I'm sitting on the couch watching the Great British Baking Show when I get a text from Jill saying, "I love you and miss you even though you hate me" and I get a text from another girl named Alejandra saying sorry, that she had told her coworker about me and how he said he'd kill to have a friend like me and I'm sitting there knowing that I'm past the part of needing validation for my healing but also happy that I finally got it.

I spent so much time trying to be what everyone else needed but never questioned why no one ever asked me what I needed. You can't find yourself looking into other people, and sometimes loneliness isn't the enemy. Sometimes it's the only thing that can help you find yourself. I've spent so much of my own life trying to build these friendships and get to know all these people without really getting to know myself. And I'm pretty great.

So no, I don't have friends. And my birthday will most likely be a party of three once again. Me, my mom, and my sister. And not because I couldn't get any friends or because I'm some big loser, but because I believe so much in friendship that I don't.

My life began when I realized I'm enough, and it's gotten better since I've realized I always have been.

-Sequoia

If I

No I didn't accidentally lose your number.
And if we haven't talked in months it was
Intentional.
Relax, I know you had issues.
Have issues.
And trust me, I want to see you happy.
I wanna see you take on those fears you've held on to
For so long.
I wanna see you melt into the form you
were always meant to maintain.
I just don't wanna be front row no more.
I don't want VIP access to the process.
I don't want intel.
I don't want first hand understanding of the
Suffering through it with you
While you figure out how to treat an individual
Like me.
I'm not perfect.
Every day I wake up and read.
I search
For ways in which I grew from tainted soil.
Uprooting it
And then
Planting new seeds for me to grow.
But we ain't coming from the same sun anymore.
I'm not selling the weight on my bones for
Cheap currency y'all offer
In the form of small talk
And the desire for a free
Full disclosure into my life,
For you to take home and compare yourself to.

Your path was dug into the dirt with force,
With one in mind.
Footprints torn between destruction and new sprouts
Was never a duet between the
Both of us.
I know you check my social media.
Faces without names you know.
And I promised to make changes.
You promised the same thing.
But I kept to it.
Stop asking me where I go and who I talk to.
It's not you, so why you
Bugging?
Begging for the words you wished I said
To you
But I'll never say?
I was transforming into a monarch
While you found seats among the sour tasting,
Bitter boned
Towns people who never found fulfillment
Beyond their diploma.
Please,
Live out your dreams.
Just stop counting me in them
Or expecting me to comment.
I couldn't care less.

Orange Peel

I'm really sorry if I was flustered before.
Said things I really didn't mean.
I hope you read this and know I still love you
Very deeply.
You're not all that bad, you know
Even though you wish you were.
So then at least you'd know why people prosecuted you
Without reason.
I think sometimes things can get really
Heavy
And you don't know what to do with all of it alone.
And maybe it seems like everyone overcame their
Hardships
And for some reason things just keep getting
Harder for you.
But I promise you that's not it.
You're not broken.
Not even close, I promise you,
So stop asking people to accept damaged goods
When you're nowhere close to that.
Everything you went through,
All the times you thought
This is it
I'll never show kindness again.
In fright that people will think I can snap.
My smile won't hold warmth anymore.
The child within is gone.
It's how the world is.
But who says you have to live by other's definition of reality.
People who grew to adapt other's minds but never gave nectar
To the birth of something new in this garden we call home.

Your mind may think the impossible
And see things that others castrate,
But why aspire to the sophistication of a rose
When you hold the light of a daffodil
Or the radiance of a sunflower?
Just as beautiful.
I know it's hard and you feel yourself slipping away
And becoming the person you think will survive.
That dreaming is over.
But I'm here to tell you—
I got you,
And I love that you run with your eyes to the sky.
I love that you laugh when things break.
I love that you hold onto people as you guide them
And you make them feel welcome in places that are foreign to them.
How you sing and dance at different tempos in your head,
And how when you hug people you're never the first to let go.
Please
Don't change that.
The sunrise is bright enough to warm us both
Enough for the passing evening
And hot enough for the burning embers of tomorrow.
It'll carry us both,
You watch,
Because it's magic you see
And it's power only glimmers for the purest of spirit.
I love you
And I know your heart.
I think you should take some time to know it too

Selective Vision

Marmalade kisses on the wooden floors.
Sunrays pooling like cream of silk.
Drink me in through your eyes.
Don't come too close or lays your fingers
Where my skin has ridges and indentations.
Naked breasts veiled with thin t shirt fabric
Tattered and stained from cheap water color.
Three day old skin.
Drunken aroma.
Speech slurred on yellow tinted canvas.
Cross legged on the floor
I'll sit all day while the guitar crows
And let the world outside run by me.
Leave me behind so that I'll have eternity
To know the real meaning of
A lasting relationship.
For the sun to be frozen in half rise and half set.
I'll rest my head on the windowsill here
And let my eyes fall into darkness.
Let my art have no audience,
No wandering eyes for me to envy.
No open hand with a burn in my mind.
A time

For my art to expel all that it's held on for years,
For nights when sleep would evade me
Onto
Blank sheets to satiate your hungry heart that
Would rob a blind mother of her child, if only.
If only
To not feel so alone,
But to meet another tortured soul who could articulate
All that you tried to meditate away
Into words to live on forever.
And to be.
To remain as a vessel for all that may have
Become a stowaway in your fractured
Peace of mind.
Lend me your paintbrush.
I must continue
For the sun has not froze,
And the pool of sun has become a flood.
Drown me in your peace.
In your want.
Your desire.
Drown me.
Drown me.

Quick Note

You know what's so crazy?
When I stopped looking for other people.
Stopped calling a witch hunt for empty bodies who I thought would never leave
And the only object in sight was a mirror.
I fell in love.
Fell in love with the person who was always here to listen
To my heart,
My doubts,
And my fears.
Why do we search for boundless love in others
When the love of our life is so near?

Foreign Energy

Solitude can be such a gorgeous experience
When it's self-induced.
When you realize your energy and heart
Don't match up with others anymore.
When your banter is no longer searched for.
When that magic you swore you felt
Subsides and the reality is that
You're nothing special,
At least not to them anymore.
They feel like they've figured you out
All the cool tricks and mysteries you carry with your
Strut and your pose.
Like little children, they've grown
Bored,
And you realize your peace of mind,
All your growth
Is not worth a small fantasy of
Human connection.
If it's not really there,
I'll slowly pull away from you.
The calls will be less frequent.
Your reach will weaken.
Roll calls will go unanswered.
My eyes will close so that
my ears can
Hear the hum of the new music I've introduced.
One day you'll wonder where I went,
Or where you went wrong.
But you didn't do anything wrong.
I just seeped into the wall lining.
Still there,
But never present enough for you to see me,
Because this next chapter in my life
Is meant for only me.

Indebted

To whom can I pay homage for crafting such a beautiful day.
For pulling the horizon with steel hooks.
For keeping the hours somber if only to keep the warmth of the sun in my
eyes a few moments more.
It is such a beautiful day today.
You can finally see the sky in all its fullness,
And yet I remain indoors,
Behind glass
On a clock that never pays enough for time.
I won't get back.

Blooming Bud

Real women have curves.
She looked in the mirror.
She looked at herself naked
For the first time.
She had always known her body.
Always dressed and undressed it.
Bathed it and lathered it with sweet smelling oils,
But she had never seen it with her own eyes
In the way he saw her body.
In the way his eyes devoured every ounce
And every imperfect bend of the hip,
With a mouth wet with indecency
And burning desire.
She looked at her body for the first time.
I didn't look at my body.
Had I felt robbed of my elevated throne to my father?
Had I given up my seat on his lap so easily?
A token feeling of not loss
But transformation.
A final pull into the index and a choice of narrative.
No longer a young girl,
But now a young woman.

Finance

You don't owe them anything.
Human decency is more than just
In your arena of proficiency.
You've taken on the bottomless burden and their urgency.
Your energy deserves rigorous protection endlessly.
Remember that you tried when they said it would never last.
Love yourself the way you love others even when you're mad.
It's sad that you wear the mask of their delusions,
And allowed yourself to be tied up in all the confusion
That they caused.
Fuck that car note,
And the fuck the responses that never came when your actions
Were clearly a cry for help—
A plea for resurrection in five minute comedic tragedies that
Held comments we won't mention.
You are more than just magic
And more than universal
To confessional hours you make feel personal.
For platonic intimacies that left you raw
To the bone and frozen gazes that never thaw.
You try and try,
But your efforts were never going to be received or
Reciprocated.
No, instead they were deceived.
The one person who offered her sleeve
Like tissue paper out of a ripped box
With not much more to give.
I saw what they did to you,
How your spirit was used as a wash rag
Made dirty.
Stop lending out your soul for external profit
Their comfortability will never be worth your peace.

Sangria

On my twentieth birthday I tacked up sheets,
Covered the walls and floors,
Threw pillows down
For a fort party at seven
Seven came
As it did every year.
The cake sat out
As it did every year.
And I stood in the middle of an empty room
And my phone more bumping than my party
With "maybe next year"
And "girl I'm sorry."
From people who barely showed
Not even the one day it counted,
But in times where they needed my comfort
A cost had never been mounted
Against them or for me
To increase exponentially
Only for my interest.
Seven thirty came
As it did every year
And I stood alone in the middle of my room
Away from my aunt and my mom,
Who couldn't bring themselves to say anything but,
"It's okay,
Next year let's just go out to eat huh."
And I sat
For the final time.

And this year
To finally cry
For every birthday I just brushed off
And attendance that people thought
Was perhaps a burden passing by,
Because for them they knew I wouldn't bat an eye
To forgive them and give a call
When the night has come to an end.
But then came the ring.
The first of a couple dings.
To five girls
Who I thought I wouldn't see
Attending a party where the only person they knew was me.
And then suddenly
It didn't feel like a mongrel of strangers.
If anything, I feared my heart was in danger
Of finding neighboring connections
In the souls that didn't just give me attention,
Didn't garner me with transactional affection,
But love and understanding that felt like a new direction.
A new life where I was included,
Where my morals and beliefs didn't have to be
Diluted

Into a palpable tonic for people to drink in.
Drink me in—
My mind,
My time,
And my words.
But never want to sit.
Sit and speak to each other instead of
At eyes that were void of anything beyond surface level.
My eyes carried me through the story of my night.
That didn't start off too bright
With these young women who laughed
And danced with their tongues.
Saunty tails of their lives.
And I was happy.
The cake was eaten
As it was every year.
The candles blown out
As they were every year.
But what was most different wasn't the end,
But finally for once
I had spent my birthday with women
Who I came to individually call
My Friends.

For Me

You are
So beautiful.
Exquisite in every frame of the word.
Reluctant in not the way you feel
Or limiting of the depth of your emotions.
You fear not the feeling of loss,
But the missing out of such encompassing feeling.
You are derived of the purest wonder
In your approach every situation with
A child's mind and a
Gentle hand.
Lovingly you caress each heart you cross paths with
And ask not what they offer,
But what loving their lives have been left without.
You never wait for the good part,
Pause for the magic.
You create it with your hands.
And from nothing you can manifest with your words
Entire palaces of indulgent fruit from your womb.
It is because of your rapport

They cannot visually see the embedded wounds on your flesh,
Cannot smell the rot beneath your breast,
Or the stained cheeks never once treated with care,
Taken without urgency
Or without respect.
You have given your all and have never
Withdrew from your lot after each double crossing.
You are the definition of unending love,
Of unmatched devotion,
And a healer for all left barren of true completion.
You are the words people cannot think to say.
You are not the problem.
You do not love too hard.
You do not give too much.
You do not do things in excess.
You are beautiful.
You are whole.
You're me.
And I am
Beautiful.

Spell Casta

I think I finally see
What objective eyes found in the seams
Of my flesh and being
A highly favored entity blessed with intense feeling.
And how I've managed to weave my words with meaning.
Spiritual healing
To gift you wisdom that's everlasting
And not force your emotional depth into a form of fasting.
Pretending you won't feel what I acknowledge to be real.
I laid awake with tears in my eyes
And my lover by my side
As he left me to be nothing more than a fly on the wall.
To believe I held no greatness at all,
But sensory pleasures he absorbed through my commentary.
Through my building him up
And drinking of my overflowing cup that took me
Months to fill.
My fingers dragging across my screen
As I practiced the final scene to relay to a panel
Of people
Who never knew my struggle to get there.
I've come to bear witness to the greatness I forgot I've always had
The drive I never took the time to see.
Feeling like I was failing.
But I am powerful.
I am patient.
And I am magic.

The Sun Came Out

This morning I tossed out of bed,
Put on my work clothes and saw
Rays of sun peeking behind my blinds.
Now I know one of y'all put that
Boo boo juju
Mal de ojo
On me.
But girl, it's a new day
Imma stop thinking that way.
Where I think if I'm not my peers' mirror
I'm somehow less
Behind in growth and progress.
For now the light in the sky
Is enough for me to realize
That there is no comparison between you and I.

Beauty

When I sit down
And let me eyes soften —
Rainwater eyes and an expansion in my being.
Perfectly still and there is no need for words
Wrapped up in cosmic embraces somewhere near here.
I hear violins playing for the days to come.
What will come to pass
But my first love.
A home in no one's name by my own.
A car that doesn't break down every imperfect dawn.
Someone asked me what I thought of this next decade,
Where I see myself going.
With everything else in mind,
My only answer—
I see beauty.
I see myself blossoming from only the water
In which I pour into myself.
My eyes growing tired from holding so much light
That it never knew to experience in all the darkness.
And a new bearing of fruit.
Seeds planted from the dead flowers I
sowed in my sleep.
And as I weep solemnly in my bed chamber
At the stroke of twelve I do not hope to be anew,
But settle in where I am and quiet the noise
For whom I am growing to be.

The Long Walk Home

And now I see the walk of truth.
How even in all aspects I will see truth in You.
I've called to You in my dire need,
And since answering so blatantly within a perceived fee no question will I feel as
I feel this growth inside of me.
I feel it in the birds outside
That chirp loudly when I am scared.
I hear it the lack of pestilence as I sleep,
seeping in my air.
I see the truth of all You bring and now I say to You,
Thank you Father on calling me even in my imprisoned point of view.
You knew my life and the way I walked.
How even just weeks ago this is not how I talked.
Never reminded to always call upon the Glory
But feel myself slipping in the need to justify with
"Sorry!"
For what a blessing it truly is.
And no inner need will I feel to justify why my Truth is the way it is,
And it was a responsibility.
One taken with an honor and need
To fill those hearts around me now
With the creator's beginning seed.
Slowly first and in time allows
The opening of their eyes.
And as I reach heights unknown
The joy will not affect just I.

The deceptions of what they believe your wisdom brings
And fear amongst their hearts among all things.
For once they realize the true love you've had
In the history books, television, word of mouth with friends
and passing fads.
No matter the person within the message and though the hate within
their homes
They truly do miss You now,
And all the glories of what they hold.
That your messages are not selective in gifts to not only
To those believed to be tattered Gold,
But that these words are more real than you know as they have never been
this old.
And as I recollect on my life without my proud testimonies
I have forever been this bold.
I write my testaments as my time grows and as the clock will tickle,
For even I will laugh and what you bring because time can cause no fickle.
And I'll clamor to hope in no fear within my mind no matter the tales
of old.
Because of this you come to me
To remind me of my mold.
And as I do this more effortlessly with the days in all that You share
within a phase.
I promise You oh Lord of mine,
The Nations Will Be Amazed
Amen

Stingy

I want all of me
For only me.
I want my mind to spill all the destinies
I wouldn't pursue
Because I was scared they'd take me from my prison
That I now protect.
The prison that is now well kept
The prison whose cellmates I wish I never meet
Let me be selfish
For once in my life.
Let me be vain
And take part in the feast that I create.
Let the version of myself in my mind
Overtake the version that people have crafted. .
A collage of traumas and tragedies that they
Dreamt I inflicted
Lead me to be conflicted.
Torn hearts that never reached my palms.
Pages in my calendar flipping faster than I can
Keep up with.
And when I looked at who I became for others
It wasn't me.
I want me.
All of me.
The parts that people told me to cut out
Because that's not the
Strength.
They wanted to latch onto.
The pain they wanted to own up to.

A strong woman with no clear boundaries.
I want my heart.
I'm not sharing it with another anymore.
Not sharing my loving—that feels so good.
My embrace that wraps you and protects you.
I wanna save all my love for myself.
I can't breathe
Beneath the weight of your desire
To build an empire on my broken dreams
That'll be swept under the rug in order to provide
And multiply the wealth for you.
I am so precious.
My way of loving is
So precious
And I've made up my mind
My loving is for me.
Cashing in my check for
I O U's
And reaping all the benefits that I know I bring.
Searching for in others for what only
I can provide.
I want me.
All of me.
To myself.
And for no one else.

Taken

And so it happened.
The blue sky over took the light
And put her soft to sleep.
Whispered in her ear that it was only for a time
She'd be back soon to rise and shine
And bring hope for a brighter tomorrow.
When the cool breeze of the night
Robs you of your largeness
And I'll be back tomorrow too.
I'm sure I'll think of all the things I have to do.
Things I should have done the day before.
And I'm sure I'll come up with impossible expectations for myself
As we all do.
And I know I'll only get a fraction of those things done.
But that's still something to be proud of
As a sunset even half full is still striking
The small works you manage to do today
Are just as wonderful and worthy of praise
As the final completion of your big picture
So soak up this rare moment of sunshine outside
For I will only envy the patterned glow we share
On the inside.
This isn't a goodbye,
Or even a farewell that's half as bright.
I only say to you, fellow passenger
Do not fall ill into this goodnight.

Self-Love

Like orange sun rays bursting from my veins,
Let me be patient.
Pray for my inner suffering and unhealed wounds
But no time to be perfect or without doubt.
Persistent growth and fatal exposure
Stand before me and tell me I'm worth more than the next.
Scream the figures.
If I invest in myself will I see immediate gratification.
Take the deal and earn a profit.
Never too proud to admit the road was hard and
Others would have passed it with golden merit.
Others would have sang a sweet melody and glided across each step.
But there's something beautiful in my breaking point.
Something thoughtful in the tears and eyes devout of hope only to be
fueled again,
Completely unmatched in its roughness and broken patterns.
The ashes of Pompeii that nurtured a new growth within its death.
Feed me with love and understanding.
Don't open your ears to my knocks.
Don't look into me without knowing I don't wish for
A silent listener.
Reach out to me not with a hand,
Not with a long embrace,
But with your final breath before you break.
Let our beings become entangled in
Self-love,
And self-hate,
And self-acceptance.

Never will I mirror the exact image you wish to project onto me
Like a moving picture and blurry features.
Obnoxiously, my nose sits in the middle of my face the way you've come to hate
A static heap will my hair be in the morning when I wake.
Too emotional and too feeling.
Sweet sickle in my mouth will my words be before I speak them
into existence.
Before I call into the universe what is already mine.
Let me be wise
And ignorant at the same time.
As Socrates was during his trials
And may you convict me of every crime I've committed against
my neighbor.
May I be imprisoned forever in my faults and learn to wear them around
my neck.
Never will they be ugly, but forever will I know them to belong to a young
girl who
Desired nothing more than the nodding of foreign heads that never cared
If she was who she's always dreamt to be or tried
So desperately to become.
Take away the hole in my heart that I've made for strangers and old
beggars of my time
Without pay in the form of reciprocation.
All that I've got.
Bury me in my own earth.
Mother nature.
Sweet sickle sunflower in my mind,

In my mouth,
In my eyes, when I turn and see who is now the present me.
The closeness and intimacy I chased for so many years.
Deepest embrace was found within.
Greatest touch circling from the receiver to the same
Creator.
Envy not of what others have become.
Their paths seducing my own into mimicry.
No possession of a skeleton key
Unlocking every outcome I could absorb from everyone else.
It'll be alright.
For love no longer alludes me.
It follows my every step,
Every leap into the unknown that promises another fracture to my
porcelain self-concept.
But now I welcome the break.
Every hard fall.
Let me break,
So that I may begin again with more
Love,
More wide smiles and sunken eyes.
A Promise
Not for perfection
But for More.

Freedom

I had a dream that I was standing in a room
Packed audience with hands not short of thunder
Quickening as I stood
Alone.
I saw my hair down and my eyes content,
Yearning for nothing more than an extension of this moment,
A chance to bottle it up and carry it wherever I go.
I found spare cash in the back pocket of my washed jeans
And a quarter in my cup holder when I needed to make the toll.
I thought I wanted consistency in places where I found patterns.
I think this poem is supposed to be about freedom
And not rebirth.
I think this poem is about my life being about me
And not waiting for Mr. Right to walk in,
Waiting for family and friends to tell me they're proud of me.
Not waiting for a partnership, but relishing in this big break I spent my
entire life building
Freedom.

Fin
The End so Far